Comptroller of the Currency
Administrator of National Banks

Activities Permissible for a National Bank, Cumulative

2011 Annual Edition

April 2012

Contents

Activities Permissible for a National Bank, Cumulative, 2011 Annual Edition

National banks may engage in activities that are part of, or incidental to, the business of banking, or are otherwise authorized for a national bank. The business of banking is an evolving concept and the permissible activities of national banks similarly evolve over time. Accordingly, this list is not exclusive; the OCC may permit national banks to conduct additional activities in the future. Any activity described in this summary as permissible for a national bank is also permissible for an operating subsidiary of a national bank. The reverse is also true: any activity described as permissible for an operating subsidiary is also permissible for the bank to engage in directly.

ACTIVITIES

General Banking Activities

Branching

- **Drop Boxes**. Placement of United Parcel Service drop boxes at nonbranch offices of a bank does not make those offices branches within the meaning of 12 USC 36 because the boxes are owned by an independent third party, have no bank identification, and may be used by the general public for nonbanking transactions. OCC Interpretive Letter No. 980 (December 24, 2003).

- **Historic Preservation**. The OCC conditioned the approval of the establishment of a branch of a national bank on the bank's execution of a Memorandum of Agreement with the State, the State Historic Preservation Officer, and the OCC. The Agreement is to facilitate the bank's efforts in preserving the historic significance of the proposed branch building. Conditional Approval No. 601 (July 23, 2003).

- **Interstate Branching**. Laws recently enacted in some states that prohibit or restrict branching by out-of-state industrial loan companies into the enacting state have t3he effect of defeating those states' laws permitting interstate de novo branching into those states by banks generally. The result is that under the Riegle-Neal Interstate Banking and Branching Efficiency Act of 1994, federal regulators cannot approve the establishment of de novo branches in such states by any out-of-state bank. OCC Interpretive Letter No. 1068 (July 28, 2006).

- **Loan Approval and Misdirected Payments at LPOs** Loan approval and the occasional receipt of misdirected loan payments from customers may take place at a loan production office (LPO) without causing it to become a branch. OCC Interpretive Letter 902 (November 16, 2000).

- **LPO/DPO/ATM Facilities Not Subject to State Branch Restrictions**. National bank LPO/DPO/ATM facilities are not "branches" subject to 12 USC 36 and state law incorporated therein. In isolation or in combination, LPOs (loan production offices), DPOs (deposit production offices), and ATMs are not branches and so are not subject to state law restrictions on branching. None of these facilities perform any of the three core functions of banking, i.e., receiving deposits, paying checks, and lending money. First National Bank of McCook v. Fulkerson, 98-D-1024 (USDC CO—March 10, 2000).

- **Remote Check-Scanning Terminal**. A remote check-scanning terminal at a customer's location, which permits the customer to deposit checks electronically, is not a branch. OCC Interpretive Letter No. 1036 (August 10, 2005).

- **Retention of Branches of Converted Federal Savings Bank**. A federal savings bank may convert to a national bank. The resulting national bank may retain all the branches of the savings bank in states where the national bank did not have branches, and the national bank may merge into an affiliated national bank and retain all the branches resulting from the previous transaction. Corporate Decision No. 2000-05 (March 28, 2000).

- **Riegle-Neal Act Interstate Merger**. Affirming the court below, the U.S. Court of Appeals for the Eighth Circuit held that the OCC's determination that the merger of a Missouri bank with a Kansas bank complied with Riegle-Neal's "minimum age" provisions for the merging banks and was entitled to deference. Riegle-Neal allows states to prohibit mergers between in-state and out-of-state banks, which have been in existence for less than five years. Missouri adopted such a law. However, the court agreed with the OCC that the Missouri law did not apply because the surviving bank's main office was in Kansas. The OCC filed an amicus brief. TeamBank, N.A. v. McClure, 279 F.3d 614 (8th Circuit 2002).

- **Underserved Communities**. A national bank may establish branches for the sole purpose of serving an underserved community, and, may acquire a noncontrolling investment a company that specializes in providing these services. Conditional Approval No. 612 (November 21, 2003).

- **Use of Trade Names**. Based on representations as to steps that would be taken to avoid customer confusion, bank's operation of branches at Wal-Mart stores under a trade name was found to be consistent with Interagency Statement on Branch Names. OCC Interpretive Letter No. 977 (October 24, 2003).

Capital

- **Asset-Backed Commercial Paper Liquidity Facility Secured by Margin Loan Facilities**. A national bank may apply a 10 percent credit conversion factor to asset-backed commercial paper (ABCP) liquidity facility backed by margin loan facilities that have no maturity or external rating, provided that liquidity facility have original maturity of one year or less. OCC Interpretive Letter No. 1099 (May 11, 2007).

- **California Registered Warrants**. The California Attorney General opined that these warrants are valid and binding obligations of the state. Interagency guidance states that because they share the same expected source of repayment, the warrants generally have the same credit quality characteristics as the state's other general obligations. For risk-based capital purposes, general obligation claims on a state receive a 20-percent risk weight. As with any obligation issued by a jurisdiction, financial institutions should exercise prudent judgment and sound risk management practices with respect to the warrants. Interagency Guidance on California Registered Warrants (July 8, 2009).

- **Conversion Factor for Asset-Backed Commercial Paper Liquidity Facility**. The following are eligibility requirements for assignment of a favorable credit conversion factor to asset-backed commercial paper (ABCP) liquidity facilities: 1) external ratings issued by Nationally Recognized Statistical Rating Organizations (NRSRO) must be published in accessible public form and monitored by the NRSRO; private ratings do not qualify; 2) if the liquidity facility supports privately rated or unrated asset-backed security (ABS), a bank may look through to the underlying assets if aging analyses and information on the relevant credit enhancements are available; 3) when the underlying assets are Organization for Economic Cooperation and Development (OECD) central government-guaranteed assets, the liquidity would be deemed eligible; and 4) in both cases, the risk weight would be subject to a 20 percent floor. OCC Interpretive Letter No. 1098 (March 1, 2007).

- **Government-Sponsored Entities (GSE) Preferred Stock**. Pursuant to the OCC's risk-based capital guidelines, preferred stock issued by a GSE falls within the meaning of the term "security" and qualifies for a 20 percent risk weight. OCC Interpretive Letter No. 964 (March 17, 2003).

- **Investment in Fannie Mae and Freddie Mac Preferred Stock**. The federal banking and thrift regulatory agencies allowed banks, bank holding companies, and thrifts to recognize the effect of the tax change enacted in section 301 of the Emergency Economic Stabilization Act of 2008 (EESA) in their third-quarter 2008 regulatory capital calculations. Section 301 of EESA provides tax relief to banking organizations that have suffered losses on certain holdings of Federal National Mortgage Association (Fannie Mae) and Federal Home Loan Mortgage Corporation (Freddie Mac) preferred stock by changing the character of these losses from capital to ordinary for federal income tax purposes. Although the EESA was not enacted until October 3, 2008, the agencies allowed banking organizations to recognize the economic benefits of the change in the tax treatment in the third quarter of 2008 for regulatory capital purposes. Attachment to OCC Bulletin 2008-31 (October 24, 2008). The agencies subsequently announced the extension of the applicability of the October 24, 2008, Interagency Statement on direct investments to certain indirect investments in Fannie Mae and Freddie Mac preferred stock. News Release 2008-129 (October 31, 2008). The Treasury Department and the Internal Revenue Service issued Rev. Proc. 2008-64 on October 29, 2008, to provide banking organizations the tax benefit of treating gains and losses on certain indirect investments in Fannie Mae and Freddie Mac preferred stock as ordinary rather than capital. Indirect investments in Fannie Mae and Freddie Mac preferred stock include certain adjustable rate preferred stock programs (such as auction pass-through certificates) and stock held by certain subsidiaries of financial institutions. News Release 2008-129 (October 31, 2008).

- **Margin Loans**. The OCC and the Federal Reserve Board issued a joint opinion that for risk-based capital purposes, a liquidity facility should be considered an eligible asset-backed commercial paper (ABCP) liquidity facility so long as the liquidity provider is only permitted to purchase margin loan facilities from the conduit at par if the market value of the collateral exceeds the outstanding loan balance by 25 percent. The risk-based capital treatment would be: apply a 10 percent credit conversion factor to the unused amount of the commitment with an original maturity of one year or less and assign a 100 percent risk weight to the resulting credit equivalent assets based on the nature of the obligor and collateral. OCC Interpretive Letter No. 1099 (May 11, 2007).

- **Margin Loans**. A national bank may use an alternative approach to calculate its capital requirement for certain eligible bank margin loans to customers for the purpose of buying or carrying margin stock. Under the alternative approach, the bank may assign a 10 percent risk weight to the principal amount of such loans provided that 1) the securities collateral of such loans are liquid and readily marketable; 2) the loans and associated collateral are marked to market daily; 3) the loans are subject to the initial margin requirements under Regulation T and daily margin maintenance requirements under NYSE Rule 431; and 4) the bank has conducted a sufficient legal review to conclude that it would be able to liquidate the collateral for the loans without undue delay, even in the event of the borrower's bankruptcy or insolvency. OCC Interpretive Letter No. 1104 (September18, 2008).

- **Merchant Processing Intangibles (MPI)**. The OCC determines that MPIs generally fail to satisfy the separability, valuation, and marketability criteria, and therefore, the list of qualifying intangible assets should not be expanded to include MPIs. Consequently, MPIs must be deducted from Tier 1 capital and assets in calculating the bank's risk based capital ratio. OCC Interpretive Letter No. 990 (October 17, 2003).

- **Mortgage Loans Modified Under the Home Affordable Mortgage Program**. The federal bank and thrift regulatory agencies issued a final rule providing that mortgage loans modified under the U.S. Department of the Treasury's Home Affordable Mortgage Program (HAMP) will generally retain the risk weight appropriate to the mortgage loan prior to modification. The agencies adopted as final their interim final rule issued on June 30, 2009, with one modification. The final rule clarifies that mortgage loans whose HAMP modifications are in the trial period, and not yet permanent, qualify for the risk-based capital treatment contained in the rule. 74 *Federal Register* 60137 (November 20, 2009).

- **Multifamily Residential Mortgage Property Annual Net Operating Income Requirements**. The actual operating income of a multifamily residential property must be used by the bank in order to determine whether the a loan secured by a first mortgage on a multifamily residential property would satisfy the annual net operating income requirements, and therefore, qualify for the 50 percent risk weight under the risk-based capital guidelines. An operating statement prepared by a qualified asset manager (not based on the actual operating income of the property) would not satisfy the annual net operating income requirements. OCC Interpretive Letter No. 989 (August 18, 2003).

- **Private Rating**. The OCC and the Federal Reserve Board issued a joint opinion that concluded that, for risk-based capital purposes, private ratings do not qualify as external-rating for purposes of determining eligibility for liquidity facilities that support asset-backed commercial paper (ABCP) conduit assets under the asset quality test. However, in the absence of an acceptable external rating, a bank may, in certain instances, look through asset-backed securities to the underlying assets to determine the eligibility of an ABCP liquidity facility. OCC Interpretive Letter No. 1098 (March 1, 2007).

- **Regulatory Capital—Alternative Approach to Calculating Risk-Based Capital for Securities Lending Transactions**. A bank may use, pursuant to the reservation of authority for case-by-case determinations contained in the OCC's risk-based capital regulations, an alternative calculation based on the bank's value at risk model (VAR approach) to determine the risk-based capital charge for certain securities lending transactions. Under the VAR approach, the risk-based capital charge would be based on a measure of economic exposure that takes into account the market value of collateral received and security lent, as well as the market price volatilities of both the securities lent by the bank and received as collateral. OCC Interpretive Letter No. 1066 (November 8, 2005).

- **Regulatory Capital—Commitment to Issue a Letter of Credit**. Under risk-based capital guidelines, a multipurpose loan commitment with an option to draw a part of the commitment only as a trade letter of credit, is subject to an off-balance sheet item credit conversion factor (CCF) based on the lower of the CCF for a commitment with the same original maturity or a trade letter of credit. However, where the sublimits for the types of credit available under the multipurpose commitment overlap, the highest CCF must be applied to the maximum draws for risk-based capital purposes. OCC Interpretive Letter No. 1049 (January 17, 2006).

- **Regulatory Capital—Multipurpose Loan Commitment**. Under risk-based capital guidelines, a bank may apply a credit conversion factor (CCF) for a multipurpose loan commitment where the borrower draws down the credit in several forms (such as a revolving loan, a term loan, or a standby letter of credit), according to the original maturity of the commitment, unless a third party asset has been identified with respect to the exercise of the commitment as a standby letter of credit. OCC Interpretive Letter No. 1057 (June 14, 2005).

- **Regulatory Capital—Structured Second Mortgages**. Second mortgages do not meet the definition of a recourse arrangement even when the first and second mortgages are made to the same borrower simultaneously. The agencies view the second mortgage as a separate transaction that does not—in and of itself—serve as a credit enhancement. OCC Interpretive Letter No. 1058 (April 20, 2005).

- **Risk-Based Capital Treatment for Bank's Exposure to IntercontinentalExchange U.S. Trust (ICE Trust).** As a result of their dealings with ICE Trust, national banks have three types of exposures: 1) counterparty credit exposure arising from cleared credit default swap transactions, 2) exposures from margin posted as collateral for the transactions, and 3) exposure from a required contribution to the clearinghouse guarantee fund. Because of the regulated nature of ICE Trust and other prudential factors, the OCC has determined that the risk-based capital treatment provided under the risk-based capital rules does not appropriately reflect the risks of transactions with ICE Trust. Therefore, the OCC has determined to use its reservation of authority at 12 CFR 3A(b) to apply a 20- percent risk weight to these three types of exposures, a risk weight the OCC believes more appropriately reflects the risk associated with these exposures. OCC Interpretive Letter No. 1116 (May 6, 2009).

- **Second Liens in Structured Mortgage Transactions.** Clarifies the joint final rule on the "Capital Treatment of Recourse, Direct Credit Substitutes, and Residual Interests in Asset Securitizations," *Federal Register*, 66 FR 59621 (November 29, 2001), and concludes that second mortgages liens will not, in most instances, constitute recourse because they generally do not function as credit enhancements. OCC Interpretive Letter No. 987 (March 17, 2003).

- **Securities Lending and Conduit Securities Lending Transitions.** A national bank may use the value-at-risk (VAR) approach to calculate a bank's risk-based capital for securities lending and conduit securities lending transactions. To be an eligible transaction, the bank must be acting as agent or intermediary in a riskless principal transaction; the transaction must be fully collateralized; any securities borrowed, lent or taken as collateral are eligible for inclusion in the trading book and are liquid and readily marketable; any securities borrowed, lent or taken as collateral are marked-to-market daily; and the transactions are subject to daily margin maintenance requirements. Before the bank may use the VAR approach to determine its risk-based capital requirements for these transactions, the OCC Examiner-in-Charge must make a determination that the bank's VAR model and risk management practices comply with certain specified conditions. The bank also will be subject to ongoing supervisory review of its model. OCC Interpretive Letter No. 1105 (September 18, 2008).

Synthetic Securitizations of Residential Mortgage Loans. Determination by the OCC and the Federal Reserve Board staff that the principles established in Joint Agency Guidance on Synthetic Collateralized Loan Obligations (November 15, 1999) and a final rule, "Capital Treatment of Recourse, Direct Credit Substitutes, and Residual Interests in Asset Securitizations," *Federal Register*, 66 FR 59621 (November 29, 2001) may be applied to a synthetic securitization. The agencies modified some of the risk management, measurement, and disclosure requirements established in their 1999 Guidance. OCC Interpretive Letter No. 988 (July 28, 2003).

- **Tax Refund Anticipation Loans.** Tax refund anticipation loans should be risk- weighted at 100 percent, as they are not directly or indirectly guaranteed by the U.S. government or its agencies and are, therefore, ineligible to receive a lower risk-weight. OCC Interpretive Letter No. 959 (February 13, 2003).

Consulting and Financial Advice

- **Financial Adviser, in General**. National banks may provide financial, investment, or economic advisory services, including advising an investment company (as defined in section 3 of the Investment Company Act of 1940). 12 USC 24(Seventh). The following are examples of these services:

    - *Adviser for Mortgage or Real Estate Investment Trusts*. National banks may serve as the advisory company for a mortgage or real estate investment trust. 12 CFR 5.34(e)(2)(ii)(I)(1).

    - *Benefits Counseling*. National banks operating subsidiary may provide Medicare and Medicaid counseling to customers and collect and disburse insurance benefit payments. Corporate Decision No. 98-13, 1999 OCC QJ LEXIS 22 (February 9, 1998).

    - *Business Services for the Bank or Its Affiliates*. National banks may furnish services for their internal operations or the operations of their affiliates, including: accounting, auditing, appraising, advertising and public relations, data processing and data transmission services, databases, or facilities. OCC Interpretive Letter No. 513, reprinted in [1990-1991 Transfer Binder] Fed. Banking L. Rep. (CCH) ¶ 83-215 (June 18, 1990).

    - *Consumer Financial Counseling*. National banks may provide consumer financial counseling. OCC Interpretive Letter No. 137, reprinted in [1981- 1982 Transfer Binder] Fed. Banking L. Rep. (CCH) ¶ 85,218 (December 27, 1979); Interpretive Ruling (July 17, 1986); OCC Interpretive Letter No. 367, reprinted in [1985-1987 Transfer Binder] Fed. Banking L. Rep. (CCH) ¶ 85,537 (August 19, 1986); 12 CFR 5.34(e)(2)(ii)(I); 12 CFR 9.101

    - *Credit Card Registration and Notification Services*. A national bank operating subsidiary may engage in credit card registration and notification services. The subsidiary would also provide other services including a price protection service, a referral service for customers to third parties who offer extended warranty programs for various products, a free credit report annually, a newsletter containing consumer credit suggestions, and reimbursement for locksmith services. Conditional Approval No. 535 (June 21, 2002).

    - *Economic Analysis*. National banks may furnish general economic information and advice, economic statistical forecasting services, and industry studies. 12 CFR 5.34(e)(5)(v)(I).

    - *Employee Benefit and Payroll Business*. A national bank may hold a noncontrolling equity investment in a company that will provide employee benefit and payroll services to small community banks and their small business customers. The investment was incidental to the bank's business because it involved preparing and conveying financial information to the bank's customers and their employees. It would also benefit the bank's small business customers by providing services to them that would not be cost efficient for those customers to provide for themselves. OCC Interpretive Letter No. 909 (May 2, 2001).

– *Employee Benefit, Compensation Advisory, and Human Resource Services*. A national bank operating subsidiary may provide employee benefit, compensation advisory and related administrative services, and other human resources services to the bank's business customers and other businesses in the bank's market area. Corporate Decision No. 2002-2 (January 9, 2002).

– *Employee Benefits*. National banks may offer employee benefit consulting services (including health benefit consulting) to corporations wishing to establish qualified benefit plans and relocation consulting for employees of a bank or its affiliates, or customers of the bank. Corporate Decision No. 98-51, 1999 OCC QJ LEXIS 28 (November 30, 1998). National bank's operating subsidiary may also provide Medicare and Medicaid counseling to customers and collect and disburse insurance benefit payments. Corporate Decision No. 98-13, 1999 OCC QJ LEXIS 22 (February 9, 1998).

– *Employee Relocation Benefit Consulting Service*. National banks operating subsidiary may provide employee relocation benefit consulting services to small- and medium-sized business customers of the bank and their employees. The service consists of financial planning and counseling, mortgage lending, and acting as a finder, each of which is a permissible banking activity. Corporate Decision No. 99-43 (November 29, 1999).

– *Financial Consulting and Advisory Services*. National banks may engage in financial consulting and advisory services for other financial institutions and the general public, including, among other things, acting as a conduit in conveying loan terms to prospective borrowers or purchasers, supplying financial information regarding a third party, or engaging on behalf of others in research in contemplation of prospective transactions. 12 USC 24(Seventh), 92a; OCC Interpretive Letter No. 238, reprinted in [1983-1984 Transfer Binder] Fed. Banking L. Rep. (CCH) ¶ 85,402 (February 9, 1982).

– *Financial Planning and Insurance*. A national bank may sell a small amount of long-term care and disability insurance and group health, medical, and dental insurance plans in connection with the comprehensive financial planning and employee benefits consulting services offered by the national bank. Letter from Julie L. Williams, Chief Counsel, dated January 19, 1999; Letter from Julie L. Williams, Chief Counsel, dated December 30, 1997.

– *Fiscal Planning Advice to Municipalities*. National banks may offer fiscal planning advice on such questions as the timing and structure of bond issues to municipalities. OCC Interpretive Letter No., 122, [1981-1982 Transfer Binder] Fed. Banking L. Rep.

(CCH) ¶ 85,203 (August 1, 1979). They may also offer financial advice regarding public offerings of debt or equity, private placements, sale-leasebacks, and purchases and sales of companies. OCC Interpretive Letter from J.T. Watson, Deputy Comptroller (July 22, 1974).

- *Human Resources Services.* National bank's operating subsidiary may provide human resources and related services to small business clients, including: acting as co-employer of customers' employees (employee "leasing"); payroll processing; employee benefits consulting and human resources administrative services; compliance administration and safety and risk management; the sale of certain insurance products to employees through an insurance agency subsidiary; and insurance-related administrative services. Conditional Approval No. 384 (April 25, 2000).

- *Investment Advisor May Hold Special Equity Interests.* A national bank operating subsidiary may receive compensation for management and performance fees in the form of a special limited interest profit allocation in the private investment funds for which it serves as investment manager and advisor. Conditional Approval No. 578 (February 27, 2003).

- *Loss Notification and Credit Monitoring Services.* A national bank may provide its customers with credit card loss notification services. This letter also approves, for the first time, providing credit scores, credit reports, and credit monitoring services to customers. It also approves providing customers with access to their Social Security, medical, and motor vehicle records as activities that are incidental to banking. OCC Interpretive Letter No. 944 (August 12, 2002).

- *Part of, or Incidental to, Investment Advisory Services.* National bank's investment management operating subsidiary may hold small interest in certain investment funds, subject to limitations, but only when the holding is necessary to conduct permissible investment advisory activities. Investors in these funds require investment advisors to hold small interests to enhance the alignment of interests between advisors and investors. Certain of the funds may contain bank-ineligible financial instruments, including equity securities. OCC Interpretive Letter No. 897 (October 23, 2000); Letter from Julie L. Williams, First Senior Deputy Comptroller and Chief Counsel, dated October 1, 1999.

- *Reporting of Officer and Employee Securities Transactions.* Certain affiliate banks are granted a waiver from Part 12's requirement that bank officers and employees who make investment recommendations or decisions for customers must report their personal transactions in securities to the bank within ten business days after the end of the calendar quarter. The letter concludes that it is the OCC's intention to administer section 12.7(a)(4) in a fashion consistent with comparable SEC Rule 17j-1, which requires such reports within thirty days after the end of the calendar quarter. OCC Interpretive letter No. 1062 (April 24, 2006).

- *Tax Services*. National banks may provide tax planning and preparation services. 12 USC 24(Seventh); 12 CFR 5.34(e)(5)(v)(J).

- **Transactional Advice, in General**. National banks may provide financial and transactional advice to customers and assist customers in structuring, arranging, and executing various financial transactions. 12 USC 24(Seventh). The following are examples of these services:

  - *Commercial Real Estate Equity Financing*. National banks may arrange for commercial real estate equity financing. OCC Interpretive Letter No. 387, reprinted in [1988-1989 Transfer Binder] Fed. Banking L. Rep. (CCH) ¶ 85, 611 (June 22, 1987); OCC Interpretive Letter No. 271, reprinted in [1983-1984 Transfer Binder] Fed. Banking L. Rep. (CCH) ¶ 85, 435 (September 21, 1983).

  - *Economic Research*. National banks may conduct financial feasibility studies. 12 USC 24(Seventh).

  - *Mergers, Acquisitions, Divestitures, Joint Ventures, Leveraged Buyouts, Recapitalizations, Capital Structurings, and Financial Transactions*. (Including private and public financings and loan syndications). 12 USC 24(Seventh). National banks may provide financial and transactional advice in connection with the previously mentioned activities. 12 CFR 9.101.

  - *Messenger Service*. A national bank may provide consulting and advisory services to deposit customers who hire independent messenger or courier services to transport banking items to and from the bank. OCC Interpretive Letter No. 1023 (February 24, 2005).

  - *"Welfare-to-Work" Counseling*. National bank's operating subsidiary may acquire a company engaged in providing government "welfare-to-work" counseling. The acquired company counsels welfare-to-work program beneficiaries on work skills and program benefits, connects them with potential employers, and handles payments from the sponsoring government agency to employers and employees participating in the program. Corporate Decision No. 2000-11 (June 24, 2000).

Corporate Governance and Structure

- **Acquisition of Assets and Assumption of Deposits**. An application by JPMorgan Chase Bank, N.A., to acquire certain assets and assume certain liabilities from the Bank of New York was approved. In connection with the exchange transaction, JPMorgan Chase acquired 339 Bank of New York branches. CRA Decision Letter No. 136 (September 15, 2006).

- **Bank Holding Company Formation**. A national bank may undertake reorganization pursuant to 12 USC 215a-2 and 12 CFR 7.2000(a), which provide a streamlined process for a national bank to form a bank holding company or for an existing holding company to acquire an unaffiliated national bank through an exchange of the bank's stock for cash or securities of the bank holding company. Corporate Decision No. 2001-21 (July 26, 2001).

- **Bank Merger Act**. The OCC, along with the other federal financial institution regulators, issued a joint opinion concluding that the Bank Merger Act is not applicable to the acquisition of a credit card portfolio containing some credit balances by a financial institution from another financial institution, provided that the credit balances represent less than 1 percent of the value of the credit card receivables transferred and the selling institution is in compliance with section 165 of the Truth in Lending Act. OCC Interpretive Letter No. 1083 (May 3, 2007).

- **Bank Ownership by Native American Tribes**. A national bank consolidated with an interim bank to effect the acquisition of the bank by a holding company that is jointly owned by a number of federally recognized Native American tribes. This is the only bank that is owned by a consortium of Indian tribes and tribal corporations. The decision contains an extensive list of special conditions, requirements, and directors' oaths that were tailored specifically for this bank because of its tribal ownership structure. Conditional Approval No. 493 (September 28, 2001).

- **Blank Check Preferred Stock**. Consistent with 12 CFR 7.2000(b), a national bank that had elected in its bylaws to be governed by California law may issue blank check preferred stock. OCC Interpretive Letter No. 921 (December 13, 2001).

- **Capital Reduction With Voluntary Liquidation**. National bank that has discontinued banking operations may reduce its permanent capital provided that the disbursement of capital is made pursuant to a plan of voluntary liquidation. Conditional Approval No. 410 (August 20, 2000).

- **CBCA Filings; Execution of Enforceable Agreements**. The OCC may determine that CBCA standards warrant a CBCA filer with the Federal Reserve to execute an enforceable agreement with the OCC. In certain circumstances, the OCC may require an agreement that imposes substantive requirements equivalent to conditions and preopening requirements that apply to a de novo bank application. Corporate Decisions 2005-08 (April 7, 2005) and 2005-09 (June 15, 2005).

- **Change in Asset Composition**. A national bank must seek prior approval from the OCC for a fundamental change in its asset composition pursuant to 12 CFR 5.53. A national bank received approval to sell all of its deposit liabilities and substantially all of its assets to an unrelated financial institution. The Federal Deposit Insurance status of the national bank was to be immediately terminated after the deposit sale, and the bank would cease its existence by merging into its nonbank affiliate pursuant to 215a-3. Conditional Approval No. 662 (October 28, 2004).

- **Change in Bank Control Pursuant to Bankruptcy Reorganization**. The OCC did not disapprove a change in control notice in connection with a proposed acquisition. The bank was a national trust bank engaged in the provision of fiduciary services to General Motors Corporation (GM) and its current and former employees. As part of the bankruptcy reorganization of GM, all of the shares of the bank's parent company were transferred to a newly formed parent corporation. The OCC required the newly formed parent to cause the bank to enter into a written operating agreement with the OCC. Conditional Approval No. 909, Change in Bank Control Act Notice in Connection with the Proposed Acquisition of Promark Trust Bank, National Association, New York, New York by NGMCO, Inc., Wilmington, Delaware (July 2, 2009).

- **Conversion of a Colorado Federal Savings Bank and Merger**. A federal savings bank owned by Bank of America Corporation applied to convert to a national bank charter. The OCC granted conditional approval for conversion of the FSB to a national bank charter and to Bank of America to acquire by merger the national bank resulting from the conversion. The transaction resulted in the retention of the bank's main office and branches and the main office of the FSB in Colorado as a branch, as well as several subsidiaries of the FSB. The OCC determined that the transaction met the age requirements of the Reigle-Neal Act, and stated that a bank's relocation from one state to another, and prior existence as a federal savings bank, did not affect its age. Conditional Approval No. 900, Countrywide Bank, FSB and Bank of America, N.A. (April 23, 2009).

- **Conversion of a Federal Savings Bank and Merger**. A federal savings bank, insured by the FDIC and wholly owned by Capital One Financial Corporation, applied to convert to a national bank and retain its main office and branches in Delaware, the District of Columbia, Maryland and Virginia. The OCC granted conditional approval for the conversion and for merger of the converted bank into Capital One, National Association. The OCC determined that the converted bank could retain all branches operated prior to the Gramm-Leach-Bliley Act on November 12, 1999, finding that relevant state statutory standards for the branch retentions were satisfied, and further that, following the merger, the acquiring bank could retain branches in Virginia, Maryland, the District of Columbia, and Delaware under state intrastate branching laws as applied to national banks with respect to the establishment of branches. The resulting bank could also retain entities owned by the FSB as operating, financial, and statutory subsidiaries, but was required to divest an indirect noncontrolling investment in limited liability companies formed by a consortium of custom home builders to assist in the group purchases of building supplies and material. Conditional Approval No. 912, Applications to convert Chevy Chase Bank, F.S.B., McLean, Virginia, to a national bank and to merge the converted bank into Capital One, National Association, McLean, Virginia (July 14, 2009).

- **Conversion of a Federal Savings Bank to a National Bank**. The OCC approved the conversion of Morgan Stanley Trust, FSB, to a national bank, Morgan Stanley Private Bank, National Association. The OCC recognized that the resulting national bank's product delivery structure would be different from that of most banks that are subject to the OCC's large bank CRA examination procedures. Therefore, the approval was conditioned on the bank periodically providing reports to the OCC describing the products, services, investments, advisory services, volunteer and other outreach efforts provided by the bank and by its direct and indirect parent companies, affiliates and subsidiaries in low and moderate income areas of the United States, outside of the bank's CRA assessment area, that were located within geographies from which the bank drew a material portion of its deposits obtained through, or facilitated by, offices of Morgan Stanley Smith Barney, LLC brokerage offices, including any deposit production offices or loan production offices located in or near the site of any of the brokerage offices. Conditional Approval Letter. No. 147 (June 28, 2010).

- **Deferred Share Units**. Deferred share units of a national bank's holding company were found to be the equivalent of stock of the bank holding company and therefore qualified as an "equivalent interest" under the qualifying share requirement of 12 USC 72. Under section 72, a national bank director is required to hold a financial stake in the operations of the bank (or its parent company) so that the director will have an incentive to be vigilant in protecting the bank's interests. The deferred share units were found to have characteristics of and to create financial incentives similar to equity interests. OCC Interpretive Letter No. 1087 (September 5, 2007).

- **Directors' Qualifying Shares**. National bank directors may meet the qualifying shares requirement under 12 USC 72 by purchasing trust preferred stock. This offers bank directors a new means of obtaining a financial stake in the bank in addition to purchasing bank stock. OCC Interpretive Letter No. 1020 (February 8, 2005).

- **Each National Bank Is a Citizen of a Single State**. The Supreme Court issued a decision on January 16, 2006, holding that a national bank is a citizen of the one state in which it maintains its main office under the National Bank Act. The Supreme Court's decision reversed a decision by the Fourth Circuit Court of Appeals that had interpreted 28 USC 1348, the special jurisdiction provision for national banks, as providing that a national bank is a citizen of each state in which the bank has a branch or other physical presence. In earlier decisions, the Seventh and Fifth Circuits had interpreted 28 USC 1348 as providing that national banks, in parity with state banks, are citizens of at most two states: the state where the bank has its main office, and the state where the bank has its principal place of business. Wachovia v. Schmidt, 546 U.S. 303, 126 S.Ct. 941, 74 U.S.L.W. 4085 (2006).

- **Election of Corporate Governance Provisions of the Model Business Corporation Act**. A national bank may adopt corporate governance provisions of the Model Business Corporation Act (MBCA) and engage in a share exchange to ensure that its newly formed parent holding company will own 100 percent of the bank. MBCA provision allowing share exchanges are not inconsistent with applicable federal banking statutes or regulations. A national bank conducting a share exchange under the MBCA must provide adequate dissenters' rights that are substantially similar, although not necessarily identical, to those in section 215a. OCC Interpretive Letter No. 891 (April 26, 2000).

- **Election of Virginia Corporate Governance Provisions**. A national bank may elect the corporate governance provisions of Virginia law and complete a share exchange in accordance with those provisions. Virginia state law allowing share exchanges is not inconsistent with applicable federal banking statues or regulations. A national bank conducting a share exchange must provide adequate dissenters' rights that are substantially similar, although not necessarily identical, to those in section 215a. OCC Interpretive Letter No. 879 (November 10, 1999).

- **Emergency Purchase and Assumption Under Bank Merger Act and Riegle-Neal Act**. The OCC approved the purchase and assumption by a national bank in North Dakota of certain assets and liabilities of a failed bank in South Dakota. The national bank in North Dakota retained a branch of the failed bank in Minnesota and immediately resold the failed bank's other assets and liabilities to a national bank in South Dakota. The transaction qualified for immediate consummation under the emergency provisions of the Bank Merger Act. Similarly, the normal requirements for an interstate acquisition under the Riegle-Neal Act did not apply when the target bank had failed. Corporate Decisions 2009-07 and 2009-08, First Dakota National Bank and Alerus Financial, N.A. (July 17, 2009).

- **Emergency Purchase and Assumption Under Bank Merger Act and Riegle-Neal Act**. The OCC approved the purchase and assumption by a national bank in Ohio of certain assets and liabilities of a failed bank in Indiana. The transaction qualified for immediate consummation under the emergency provisions of the Bank Merger Act. Similarly, the normal requirements for an interstate acquisition under the Riegle-Neal Act did not apply when the target bank had failed. The OCC also approved the Ohio national bank's purchase and assumption of certain assets and liabilities of a failed federal savings bank in Indiana and retention of its branches. Although the federal savings bank was not a "bank" for purposes of the Riegle-Neal Act, the interstate purchase and assumption was authorized by 12 USC 24(Seventh). Retention by the Ohio national bank of the failed federal savings banks branches in several states was also approved. Retention of branches in one state was authorized by 12 USC 36, while the FDIC used its authority under 12 USC 823(k) to approve the retention of branches in other states. Corporate Decision 2009-17, First Financial Bank, N.A. (September 18, 2009).

- **Expansion of Scope of Trust Company Activities**. An application to expand the scope of activities of HSBC Trust Company, N.A. from a limited purpose trust company to include loans and deposits related to tax refunds was preliminarily approved on a conditional basis. Expansion to a full service charter subjects the bank to the Community Reinvestment Act. Conditions include, among other items, obtaining federal deposit insurance and establishing a mystery shopper program and a comprehensive compliance program for the bank's refund anticipation loan program. CRA Decision Letter No. 137 (September 29, 2006).

- **FDIC-Guaranteed Senior Unsecured Debt Under the Temporary Liquidity Guarantee Program**. The exemption from registration under Section 16.5(a) is applicable to FDIC-guaranteed senior unsecured debt that matures on or before June 30, 2012, the expiration date of the FDIC's guarantee under the Temporary Liquidity Guarantee Program. The exemption would not apply to such debt with a maturity that extends beyond June 30, 2012. OCC Interpretive Letter No. 1108 (January 26, 2009).

- **Healthcare Receivables Management.** A bank received approval to establish an operating subsidiary to offer services to manage healthcare receivable and disbursement processes, and to assist employers, insurers and third party administrators with benefits administration. A healthcare receivables manager service that automates the case application process for bank customers who are healthcare providers, such as doctors and hospitals, and provides them with an electronic remittance system to expedite payments, is a financial processing activity and thus is permissible as part of or incidental to the business of banking. Corporate Decision No. 2006-05 (June 16, 2006).

- **Inflatable Charters.** Through the filing of a change in bank control notice, the OCC will not disapprove a change in ownership or control of an existing national bank. Similar to the shelf charter concept, this is another tool used by the OCC to expand the pool of qualified bidders for troubled and failed national banks. New ownership's plans could include repositioning the assets and liabilities of the bank through a purchase and assumption, downsizing, or relocating to a suitable market. The OCC imposed certain safeguards on the new owners and the bank in order to protect the safety and soundness of the national bank. Conditional Approval No. 872 (August 27, 2008).

- **Internal Reorganization and Consolidation of Banking and Credit Card Operations.** Citigroup, Inc. in a series of twelve different applications and notices that included changes in bank control, mergers and thrift conversions internally restructured a number of its affiliates. The result was the consolidation of the domestic commercial and retail banking operations into Citibank, N.A., New York, New York, and the relocation of the head office to Las Vegas. Also, the restructure resulted in the credit card operations being consolidated into Citibank (South Dakota), N.A, Sioux Falls, South Dakota. Corporate Decision No. 2006-08 (August 3, 2006).

- **International Trade Management Services by an Operating Subsidiary.** As part of an OCC approval of the acquisition of a corporation as an operating subsidiary of a national bank, the agency found that a number of international trade-related services were either part of, or incidental to, the business of banking. The corporation's activities include maintaining a database of trade-related information for customer access and providing global supply chain management services to customers. Corporate Decision 2005-02 (March 24, 2005).

- **Internet Banking Services.** A bank received approval to establish a wholly owned operating subsidiary to provide Internet access, including dial-up ISP, to its customers and nonbank customers as part of its package of Internet banking services. It may not sell ISP services to nonbank customers unless it demonstrates regulatory compliance and obtains the OCC's prior approval. Conditional Approval No. 733 (February 16, 2006).

- **Interstate De Novo Branch Approval Based on Reciprocity Applicable to a Predecessor Bank.** The OCC approved the establishment of a de novo branch in Rhode Island by a Delaware national bank. Because the Delaware national bank was the resulting bank of a merger that included a national bank in Maine, and Maine and Rhode

Island allow reciprocal interstate branching, establishment of the branch was found to be permissible. Corporate Decision 2009-19, TD Bank, N.A. (October 22, 2009).

- **Interstate Merger Under 12 USC 215a.** The OCC conditionally approved an application to merge Bank Midwest, National Association, Kansas City, Missouri, with and into Armed Forces Bank, National Association, Fort Leavenworth, Kansas. The OCC determined that the merger qualified as a merger of banking associations located within the same state under 12 USC 215a, because both the Armed Forces Bank main office and a branch of Bank Midwest were located in Kansas. The OCC also determined that the financial and managerial resources of the banks and their future prospects were consistent with approval of this merger, as provided for under the Bank Merger Act, because the transaction would result in a substantial influx of capital to the resulting bank, along with Bank Midwest's entire allowance for loan and lease losses and other beneficial results, allowing Armed Forces Bank to continue to serve military personnel on their bases and customers at lower-cost branch sites. Conditional Approval No. 980 (November 15, 2010).

- **Issuance of Common Stock Below Par Value.** A national bank may issue shares of its common stock at an issue price less than its par value. The assessment provisions of 12 USC 55 for a deficiency in capital do not apply to the transaction, provided that: (i) applicable corporate governance procedures permit such issuance, and (ii) the bank takes appropriate measures to ensure that any below par sale will not cause its capital stock to become impaired. OCC Interpretive Letter No. 1112 (February 17, 2009).

- **Kansas State Rehabilitation Tax Credits.** A bank received approval to establish an operating subsidiary to facilitate the purchase of Kansas State Rehabilitation Tax Credits. Purchasing, holding, and subsequently selling transferable state tax credits are permissible activities for national banks. A severely circumscribed limited partnership interest could be acquired by the subsidiary when needed to facilitate the bank's participation in permissible financial intermediary activities. Corporate Decision 2006-6 (July 12, 2006).

- **Limited Equity Investment in Connection With Investment Management Activities.** A bank received conditional approval for its operating subsidiary to hold for limited periods of time a limited interest in a private investment fund for which it serves as investment manager. Performance-based compensation structured as an allocation to the investment manager is recognized industry practice. Conditions require, among other items, a risk management process and restriction to certain types of instruments. Conditional Approval Letter No. 755 (August 25, 2006).

- **Loan Restructure and Creation of Operating Subsidiaries.** Through a merger, a national bank acquired large commercial loans outstanding to the affiliates of credit management corporation. The corporation serviced mortgage loans originated and purchased by the affiliates. The commercial loans were collateralized by the mortgage loans, other real estate owned (OREO) as the result of foreclosures, and stock of the credit management corporation. The bank proposed to restructure the commercial loans, which were under forbearance agreements, in order to acquire control over the underlying mortgages and underlying OREO, retaining the credit management corporation as the servicer. The bank's expectation was to be better able to mitigate potential loan losses, to benefit the affiliates' customers through loss mitigation strategies, and to realize tax benefits. The OCC issued a preliminary conditional approval for a series of transactions to result in the creation of three operating subsidiaries—a statutory trust to hold the bank's interest in the underlying mortgage loans and OREO; a limited liability company wholly owned by the bank's existing real estate investment trust, to receive net collections; and a OREO subsidiary to the limited liability company—and an associated nonmaterial noncash contribution from the bank's holding company. The approval was based in part on bank authority to take real estate in satisfaction of debts previously contracted. Conditional Approval No. 895, The Huntington National Bank (March 31, 2009).

- **Merger of Holding Company into Subsidiary National Bank**. A national bank owned by a holding company may eliminate its holding company by merging the holding company into the national bank. The merger must be permissible for the holding company under the state law of the state in which the holding company is incorporated. The merger is permissible for national banks under 12 USC 215a-3. Corporate Decision No. 2001-33 (November 29, 2001).

- **Merger of Mortgage Banking Companies Into a Bank Under the AHOEO Act**. A national bank's mortgage banking subsidiary and the mortgage banking subsidiary of one of its affiliate banks may merge directly into the national bank, under American Home Ownership and Economic Opportunity Act of 2000 section 1206, 12 USC 215a-3, which permits mergers between national banks and non-national bank subsidiaries and affiliates, subject to OCC approval. Corporate Decision No. 2001-22 (July 26, 2001).

- **Merger of a National Bank Into Nonbank Affiliate**. A national bank may cease its existence as a national bank by merging into a nonbank affiliate as authorized under 12 USC 215a-3 and the OCC's recently adopted regulation at 12 CFR 12 CFR 5.33(g)(5). The merger must be permissible for the nonbank affiliate under state law. The national bank may not be an insured bank at the time of the merger. Corporate Decision No. 2004-8 (March 15, 2004).

- **Merger of National Trust Bank Into Nonbank Affiliates**. A national trust bank may terminate its activities and cease operations through a series of transactions as granted under the authority provided under 12 USC 215a-3 and the OCC's recently adopted regulation at 12 CFR 5.33(g)(5). Corporate Decision No. 2004-7 (March 31, 2004).

- **Share Reclassification Pursuant to Tennessee State Corporate Law**. A national bank that has elected Tennessee law as its corporate governance process under 12 CFR 7.2000(b) may reclassify common stock held by the bank's shareholders into new classes of preferred stock in accordance with Tennessee law. Before effecting the share reclassification, the bank must file an application under 12 CFR 5.46 and receive the OCC's approval. OCC Interpretive Letter No. 1125 (February 11, 2001).

- **Shelf Charter**s. The OCC issued preliminary conditional approvals for a number of shelf charters, for the purpose of assuming liabilities and purchasing assets from the Federal Deposit Insurance Corporation (the FDIC) acting as the receiver of a depository institution. Because only chartered depository institutions may assume deposit liabilities from the FDIC, this structure provides investors in the bank holding company owning the shelf charter the opportunity to assume liabilities and purchase assets from the FDIC as receiver of a depository institution. Since the bank does not commence operations until after its bid for a particular institution is accepted by the FDIC, the specific size, scope, and activities of the bank are not determined until it acquires the business of a specific failed institution. OCC approvals are based upon the information provided by the bank, including the experience of proposed key management. A shelf charter must follow an organizing process that includes OCC review as it considers potential acquisition transactions. It is anticipated that the OCC will grant final approval for such a bank and will approve a purchase and assumption transaction under the Bank Merger Act the first time that the bank's bid to acquire a failed institution is accepted by the FDIC. Final approval and authorization for the proposed bank to open is not granted until all pre-opening requirements are met. The OCC requires a written Operating Agreement requiring the bank comprehensive business plan acceptable to the OCC. Conditional Approval No. 905, Application to establish a new national bank, with the title of Carlile Bank, National Association (May 29, 2009); Conditional Approval No. 917, Application to establish a new national bank, with the title of SJB National Bank (July 31, 2009); Conditional Approval No. 922, NewBank National Association (August 28, 2009); Conditional Approval No. 936, Application to establish a new national bank, with the title of Bond Street Bank, National Association (October 23, 2009).

- **"Shelf Charter" Initial Use to Acquire Failed Banks**. The OCC approved the acquisition of failed banks by two national bank established under "shelf charters." Bond Street Bank, National Association, was granted preliminary approval as a shelf charter in 2009. In January 2010, the OCC granted final approval for the bank to establish Premier America Bank, National Association, which acquired Premier American Bank, a state-chartered bank closed by the Florida Department of Financial Services, Division of Banking. The OCC approved the acquisition of a second failed Florida state bank by Premier America Bank, National Association later that month. In July, the OCC approved the acquisition of two Florida banks and one South Carolina bank by a bank established under another shelf charter, NAFH National Bank. Conditional Approval Letter No. 944 (January 22, 2010); Conditional Approval Letter No. 945 (January 29, 2010); Conditional Approval Letter No. 960 (July 16, 2010).

- **Wholesale Bank to Hold Deposits Generated from Deposit Sweep Arrangements**. The OCC issued a preliminary conditional approval for the chartering of a wholesale bank to hold deposits generated from deposit sweep arrangements with its affiliated broker-dealers, including Merrill Lynch, Pierce Fenner & Smith Inc. and, possibly, unaffiliated entities. Although the deposits that bank will hold will be beneficially owned by the individual brokerage customers, and will be covered by pass-through FDIC deposit insurance, the bank will have a direct contractual relationship in the form of a deposit agreement only with the broker-dealers that offer the deposit sweep product, not with the individual customers. The bank will also participate in various lending facilities offered by the Federal Reserve banks, primarily TAF (Term Auction Facility) and Fed Funds, to provide an additional source of funding for its affiliates. In addition, the bank will acquire mortgage loans (i.e., one- to four-family residential and home equity lines of credit) and/or mortgage-backed securities from its insured bank affiliate, Bank of America, N.A. (BANA), and hold them on its balance sheet in order to maintain the appropriate capital ratios. Conditional Approval No. 899, Bank of America N.A., (April 23, 2009).

- **Operating Subsidiaries, in General**

  – A national bank may establish an operating subsidiary offering various services for customers engaged in capital gains tax-deferred exchanges of real and personal business or investment property, known as "like-kind exchanges," under Internal Revenue Code 26 USC 1031. The subsidiary may provide advisory services, make referrals to third-party providers, and serve as a qualified intermediary or exchange accommodation titleholder. Financial and investment advisory services are permissible activities for national banks and their operating subsidiaries, and the referral of customers to third-party providers is a permissible finder activity. The provision of qualified intermediary and exchange accommodation titleholder services is considered incidental to the business of banking. Conditional Approval No. 869 (July 22, 2008).

- **Operating Agreement**. The OCC conditionally approved a merger application involving two uninsured trust banks requiring that, prior to consummation, the resulting uninsured national bank enter into an operating agreement with the OCC. The operating agreement required the bank to: 1) provide the OCC with periodic strategic plans to include specific, measurable, and verifiable performance objectives, 2) maintain at least certain minimum levels of capital and liquid assets, and 3) enter into a capital assurance and liquidity maintenance agreement with its parent. Should the bank fail to meet the terms of the operating agreement, the bank would be required to submit a: 1) remedial action plan with modified objectives and a timeframe and implementation strategy, or 2) contingency plan to sell, merge, or liquidate the bank. Conditional Approval No. 624 (February 20, 2004).

- **Reduction of Par Value**. A national bank may reduce the par value of its shares to $0.01 per share with an offsetting increase to the bank's capital surplus. The reduction in par value may reduce the bank's state franchise taxes. OCC Interpretive Letter No. 963 (April 14, 2003).

- **Reorganizations, in General**

  – A national bank and certain affiliates may combine and reorganize their banking and trust business lines to effect a separation of two principal business lines into two different institutions. Conditional Approval No. 859 (June 13, 2008).

- A state Industrial Loan Company (ILC) may convert to a national bank under 12 USC 35 and 214(a) so long as the industrial bank or industrial loan company is a banking institution under state law and is engaged in the business of receiving deposits. Conditional Approval No. 880 (September 21, 2008).

- **Restructuring of Credit Card, International, Consumer, and Commercial Finance Businesses**. A banking organization's credit card, international, consumer, and commercial finance businesses were restructured in a large, complex transaction. The restructuring resulted in one bank being the main issuer of consumer credit cards, and another bank being the issuer of government, corporate, and certain consumer credit cards. As part of this transaction, various ancillary entities that were bank or holding-company subsidiaries became subsidiaries of the credit card-issuing banks. Certain activities related to ownership of motor vehicles were approved for the first time, either as finder activities or on an excess capacity basis. Newly authorized finder activities included assisting vehicle owners in selling their vehicles; assisting them in locating tow trucks and vehicle repair facilities; assisting corporate customers in obtaining employee driving records from the state motor vehicle department; and assisting such customers with driver's license renewals and vehicle registrations. Newly authorized excess capacity activities included management of third-party subrogation claims for accidents involving automobiles not leased from the bank, and assisting owners of vehicle fleets in establishing corporate safety policies. In addition, certain finance company affiliates were transferred to and became subsidiaries of one of the banks. Corporate Decision No. 2001-28 (September 21, 2001).

- **Retention of a Noncontrolling Investment in a Financial Services Holding Company Following the Conversion of the Holding Company's Wholly Owned Subsidiary From a State Limited Commercial Bank Charter to a National Bank Charter**. Because the standards in 12 CFR 5.36 for noncontrolling investments appeared to be satisfied, existing national bank shareholders of a financial services holding company could retain their noncontrolling investments following the conversion of a holding company subsidiary from a state limited commercial bank charter to a national bank charter. The subsidiary would continue to operate primarily as a provider of correspondent services to community banks but would not qualify as a banker's bank because of its current and proposed activity of making direct commercial loans to nonbank customers. OCC Interpretive Letter No. 1092 (March 22, 2007).

- **Reverse Stock Split**. Pursuant to 12 CFR 5.46, a national bank in California may elect the corporate governance provisions of Delaware and complete a reverse stock split in accordance with those provisions. The approval is subject to conditions that the bank provide for dissenters' rights comparable to those found in 12 USC 214a, 215, and 215a, and pay the cost of any appraisal (but not attorneys' or experts' fees) that might occur if a shareholder dissents. Conditional Approval No. 670 (December 27, 2004).

- **Reverse Stock Split**. Consistent with 12 CFR 7.2000(b) and 7.2023, a national bank in Mississippi may elect the corporate governance provisions of Mississippi law and complete a reverse stock split with those provisions. Conditional Approval No. 562 (December 9, 2002).

- **Reverse Stock Split**. Consistent with 12 CFR 7.2000(b) and 7.2023, a national bank in Alabama may elect the corporate governance provisions of Alabama law and complete a reverse stock split in accordance with those provisions. Conditional Approval No. 541 (July 30, 2002).

- **Reverse Stock Split, Delaware and Kentucky Corporate Governance Procedures**. The OCC granted approvals of reverse stock splits conducted under Delaware and Kentucky corporate governance procedures for the first time. A list of states where the OCC has approved reverse stock splits under the respective state's corporate governance procedures is contained in the Capital and Dividends booklet of the *Comptroller's Licensing Manual*. Conditional Approval No. 670 and 683 (December 27, 2004 and April 7, 2005).

- **Shelf Charters**. The OCC will grant conditional, preliminary approval to a "shelf charter," designed to facilitate new equity investment in troubled depository institutions. The charter remains inactive, or "on the shelf" until such time as the investor group is in a position to acquire a troubled institution. By granting the preliminary approval, the OCC expands the pool of potential buyers available to buy troubled institutions, and in particular the equity capital made available to bid on troubled institutions through the Federal Deposit Insurance Corporation's bid process. The approval requires a streamlined business plan that describes how the acquired bank will be operated. The OCC can later grant conditional preliminary approval of a national bank charter, subject to certain conditions and to requirements that more detailed operating plans, satisfactory to the OCC, be submitted, if the bank targets a specific institution for acquisition. News Release 2008-137 (November 21, 2008). See also Conditional Preliminary Approval Letter (November 17, 2008).

- **Share Exchange**. A national bank may effect a share exchange to become a subsidiary of a bank holding company pursuant to 12 USC 215a-2 and 12 CFR 7.2000, by offering most shareholders holding company stock, but providing cash to out-of-state residents, to avoid costs associated with registering its stock under the Securities Act of 1933. Corporate Decision No. 2002-08 (May 15, 2002).

- **Termination of National Bank Activities**. A national bank may terminate its activities, and cease operations through a series of transactions including those granted under the authority provided under 12 USC 215a-3. The bank ceased its deposit-taking activities, caused FDIC to cancel its status as an insured depository institution, and an affiliated bank acquired its remaining assets through a 215a-3 merger. Corporate Decision No. 2003-12 (November 26, 2003).

- **Transfer of Mortgage Servicing Business**. National banks may acquire mortgage servicing rights from an affiliate, subject to certain conditions. OCC Interpretive Letter No. 1130 (March 10, 2011).

- **Trust Company Organized as LLC**. Conversion to National Bank. A state bank organized as a limited liability company may convert to a national bank under 12 USC 35. After the conversion, the trust company would continue to follow the state limited liability company law for its internal guidance to the extent not inconsistent with applicable federal banking statutes and regulations or bank safety and soundness, under 12 CFR 7.2000. Conditional Approval No. 696 (June 6, 2005).

Correspondent Services

- **Correspondent Services, in General**. National banks may hold deposits for other banks and perform correspondent services for those banks, such as check clearing. Other examples of correspondent services are:

  - *ATM Sales to Other Banks and ATM Services*. National banks may purchase ATMs for resale to other banks, which will be in the same shared network, convert their own ATMs into a shared network, and provide services for other banks in the network. OCC Interpretive Letter (October 2, 1975); No-Objection Letter No. 87-11, [1988-1989 Transfer Binder] Fed. Banking L. Rep. (CCH) ¶ 84,040 (November 30, 1987).

  - *Disaster Relief Services*. National banks may market disaster relief services to other banks, including sharing of premises and data processing equipment. OCC Interpretive Letter (June 13, 1990).

  - *Electronic Imaging Services*. National banks may provide electronic imaging services to banks and other financial firms. OCC Interpretive Letter No. 805, reprinted in [1997-1998 Transfer Binder] Fed. Banking L. Rep. (CCH) ¶ 81-252 (October 9, 1997).

  - *Financial and Consulting Services*. National banks may offer financial and consulting services, including market research and analysis, strategic planning, advertising and promotion planning, product development, personnel management, employee relations, affirmative action, and salary and benefit plans to banks and commercial customers. OCC Interpretive Letter No. 137, reprinted in [1981-1982 Transfer Binder] Fed. Banking L. Rep. (CCH) ¶ 85,218 (December 27, 1979).

  - *Flood Hazard Determinations*. A national bank may establish an operating subsidiary that makes flood hazard determinations for the bank, its affiliates, and unaffiliated mortgage lenders. Corporate Decision No. 97-79, 1998 OCC QJ LEXIS 6 (July 11, 1997).

  - *Internal Security Consulting Services*. National banks may provide internal security consulting services, including security and guard services at affiliate banks and non-national bank affiliates and may install and maintain vaults, locks, and ATMs for third-party banks. OCC Interpretive Letter No. 398, reprinted in [1988-1989 Transfer Binder] Fed. Banking L. Rep. (CCH) ¶ 85,622 (September 28, 1987).

– *Investment Portfolio Management Service.* A national bank may establish an operating subsidiary to provide investment portfolio management services and computer networking services for the bank and other financial institutions. OCC Interpretive Letter No. 754, reprinted in [1996-1997 Transfer Binder] Fed. Banking L. Rep (CCH) ¶ 81,118 (November 6, 1996).

– *Loan Collection and Repossession Services.* National banks may offer loan collection and repossession services for other banks and thrifts. OCC Interpretive Letter (December 14, 1983); OCC Interpretive Letter (March 15, 1971).

– *Other Correspondent Services.* National banks may print and market checks, drafts, loan payment coupons, and other banking documents; perform tax planning and tax preparation assistance; and perform financial data processing for correspondent banks. OCC Interpretive Letter (February 11, 1980); OCC Interpretive Letter (October 14, 1975).

– *Payment and Information Processing Services.* National banks may establish an operating subsidiary that engages in payment and information processing services. The subsidiary may own/operate/sell electronic data processing and data interchange facilities, which will be used to communicate billing and payment-related information to insurance carriers responsible for paying for medical benefits. The subsidiary may provide computer network services, including necessary hardware to financial institutions. Corporate Decision No. 98-12, 1998 OCC QJ LEXIS 130 (February 9, 1998); OCC Interpretive Letter No. 712, reprinted in [1995-1996 Transfer Binder] Fed. Banking L. Rep. (CCH) ¶ 81-027 (February 29, 1996); OCC Interpretive Letter No. 718, reprinted in [1995-1996 Transfer Binder] Fed. Banking L. Rep. (CCH) ¶ 81-033 (March 14, 1996). National banks may also provide lockbox services. OCC Interpretive Letter No. 635, reprinted in [1993-1994 Transfer Binder] Fed. Banking L. Rep. (CCH) ¶ 83,519 (July 23, 1993). National banks may perform processing of county tax assessments, tax bills, and water and sewer bills. OCC Interpretive Letter (April 15, 1975).

– *Vault Cash.* A national bank may establish a correspondent account at an unaffiliated bank in another state to provide vault cash for the bank's customers in the state. OCC Interpretive Letter No. 796, reprinted in [1997 Transfer Binder] Fed. Banking L. Rep. (CCH) ¶ 81,223 (August 18, 1997).

Finder Activities

- **Transaction Finders, in General.** National banks may serve as finders for certain goods and services, i.e., they may bring parties together for a transaction that the parties themselves negotiate and consummate. 12 USC 24(Seventh); 12 CFR 7.1002. National banks may advertise and accept fees for their finder services. Finder activities include, but are not limited to, identifying potential parties, making inquiries as to interest, making introductions or arranging meetings of interested parties and otherwise bringing parties together for a transaction that the parties themselves negotiate and consummate. The following are examples of these services:

  - *Acting as Finder by Hosting Commercial Web Site for Small Retailers.* National banks may host commercially enabled Web sites for small retailers as a form of electronic "finder" activity. OCC Interpretive Letter No. 856, reprinted in, [Current Transfer Binder] Fed. Banking L. Rep. (CCH) ¶ 81-313 (March 5, 1999).

  - *Acting as Finder for Automobile Club.* National banks may sell memberships as agent for an automobile club. No Objection Letter No. 89-02, reprinted in [1989-1990 Transfer Binder] Fed. Banking L. Rep. (CCH) ¶ 83, 014 (April 17, 1989).

  - *Acting as Finder for Automobile Sales.* National banks may act as finders for automobile sales and financing through databases, call centers, and Internet services. 12 CFR 7.1002 and 7.1019; OCC Interpretive Letter No. 741, reprinted in [1996-1997 Transfer Binder] Fed. Banking L. Rep. (CCH) ¶ 81-105; Corporate Decision No. 97-60 (July 1, 1997).

  - *Acting as Finder for Automotive Roadside Assistance Programs.* A national bank may acquire operating subsidiaries that operate and administer automotive roadside assistance programs and that provide credit card registration and notification services. The bank can administer and operate auto roadside assistance programs for third parties as permissible finder activities; and can administer and operate a separate roadside assistance program, made available to its credit card customers, as an incidental activity that is convenient and useful to the administration and operation of the programs for third parties. Conditional Approval No. 535 (June 21, 2002).

  - *Acting as Finder for Government Entities.* National banks may provide electronic finder, custodian, record keeping, and financial agent services primarily to government entities. Permissible activities include providing a financial and banking data match program to enable states to match data on delinquent, noncustodial parents; an Internet-based electronic service that provides a catalog of services of state or federal agencies available to the public; and electronic service for state governments to process motor vehicle title applications and related payments via the Internet; and the operation of a backup call center for a federal agency. Conditional Approval No. 361 (March 3, 2000).

– *Acting as Finder for Health Care Programs.* National banks may provide medical insurance cost information, benefits counseling, premium collection and disbursement and related activities. OCC Corporate Decision No. 98-13, 1999 OCC QJ LEXIS 22 (February 9, 1998).

– *Acting as Finder for Insurance.* National banks may provide finder services in connection with insurance products and services. To identify permissible national bank finder arrangements in the insurance context (as an alternative to section 92 authority), the OCC considers; 1) the scope of the proposed activities; 2) the existence or absence of another insurance agent or broker in the arrangement; 3) whether the bank has a contractual relationship with an insurance company for selling its products, and if so, the nature of relationship with an insurance company for selling its products, and if so, the nature of the relationship; and 4) the bank's compensation arrangement for the proposed activities. For example, national banks may participate in sharing arrangements with other banks whereby they combine their efforts to use the services of a group of independent agencies that would solicit and sell insurance services to bank customers on site, sharing pro rata in referred business. OCC Interpretive Letter No. 824, reprinted in, [1997-1998 Transfer Binder] Fed. Banking L. Rep. (CCH) ¶ 81-273 (February 27, 1998).

– *Acting as Finder for Internet Vendors.* National banks may provide to their customers links to nonbanking, third-party vendors' Internet Web site. 12 CFR 7.1002; Conditional Approval No. 221 (December 4, 1996); OCC Interpretive Letter No. 611, reprinted in [1992-1993 Transfer Binder] Fed. Banking L. Rep. (CCH) ¶ 83, 449 (November 23, 1992).

– *Acting as Finder for Investment Advisory Services.* National banks may act as finder by referring bank customers to investment advisors. OCC Interpretive Letter No. 850 (January 27, 1999), reprinted in [Current Transfer Binder] Fed. Banking L. Rep. (CCH) ¶ 83,202 (May 18, 1990); OCC Interpretive Letter (January 20, 1988).

– *Acting as Finder for Nonfinancial Products.* Under its authority to act as a finder, a national bank may help arrange for the purchase of nonfinancial products by its credit card customers. The bank proposed to make each customer who contacts the bank's call center aware that a nonfinancial product is available to the customer and that the bank will, upon the customer's request, transmit certain information to the product's vendor. OCC Interpretive Letter No. 904 (January 18, 2001).

– *Sale and Support of Credit Card Incentive Plans.* A national bank operating subsidiary may sell access to its existing credit card promotional reward points program to unaffiliated third party merchants. The merchants will purchase an inventory of the program's reward points and award them to their own customers, employees or other parties. The points will be redeemed from a merchandise/services catalog administered by the national bank operating subsidiary. Corporate Decision No. 2003-10 (June 27, 2003).

Leasing

- **Leasing, in General**. National banks may engage in personal property leasing activities under two separate authorities, 12 USC 24(Seventh) and 12 USC 24(Tenth).

  - *CEBA Leases*. A national bank may invest in tangible personal property, including vehicles, manufactured homes, machinery, equipment, or furniture, for the purpose of, or in connection with leasing that property, if the aggregate book value of the property does not exceed 10 percent of the bank's consolidated assets and the related lease is a conforming lease. 12 USC 24(Tenth). OCC Interpretive Letter No. 770, reprinted in [1996-1997 Transfer Binder] Fed. Banking L. Rep. (CCH) ¶ 81,134 (February 10, 1997). National banks may also engage in lease financing if the lease is the functional equivalent of a loan under section 24(Seventh). The OCC has interpreted this to mean that section 24(Seventh) leases must be net, full-payout leases. Under this requirement, national banks may rely on the estimated residual value only to a limited extent, i.e., the unguaranteed portion of the estimated residual value relied upon by the bank, plus the estimated cost of financing the property, must not exceed a specified percentage of the original cost of the property to the lessor. 12 CFR 23.

  - *Consulting Services Relating to Leasing*. National banks may engage in property leasing activities through a subsidiary, including lease consulting services, finder services, and lease servicing. OCC Interpretive Letter No. 567, reprinted in [1991-1992 Transfer Binder] Fed. Banking L. Rep. (CCH) ¶ 83,337 (October 29, 1991); 12 CFR 5.34(e)(2)(ii)(M).

  - *Data Processing Equipment Leasing*. National bank's operating subsidiary may enter into a general partnership with a corporation for the leasing of electronic data processing equipment on a net, full-payout basis. OCC Interpretive Letter No. 369, reprinted in [1985-1987 Transfer Binder] Fed. Banking L. Rep. (CCH) ¶ 85,539 (September 25, 1986).

  - *DPC Property Leases*. National banks may enter into a lease agreement regarding Debt Previously Contracted (DPC) property, subject to conditions and limitations. OCC Interpretive Letter No. L-5, reprinted in [1977-1978 Transfer Binder] Fed. Banking L. Rep. (CCH) 85,022 (September 2, 1977); 12 USC 29(First).

  - *Equipment and Personal Property Leasing*. National banks may invest in tangible personal property, including without limitation, vehicles, manufactured homes, machinery, equipment, or furniture, for lease financing transactions on a net lease basis, provided the aggregate book value of all such property does not exceed 10 percent of the consolidated assets of the bank. 12 USC 24(Seventh); 12 CFR 23.7; OCC Interpretive Letter No. 567, reprinted in [1991-1992 Transfer Binder] Fed. Banking L. Rep. (CCH) ¶ 83, 337 (October 29, 1991); OCC Interpretive Letter No. 556, reprinted in [1991-1992 Transfer Binder] Fed. Banking L. Rep. (CCH) ¶ 83,306 (August 6, 1991).

–   *Excess Space.* National banks may lease excess space on bank premises to other businesses, share space with other businesses, or offer its services in space owned or leased to other businesses. 12 CFR 7.3001.

–   *Lease Financing, Historic Preservation.* National banks can establish operating subsidiaries to acquire a leasehold interest in historic buildings and thus acquire the tax credits associated with those buildings. This allows the bank to reduce the borrower's costs of financing the rehabilitation and at the same time earn an improved return. The substance of this type of transaction is a financing. Corporate Decision No. 99-07, 1999 OCC QJ LEXIS 97 (March 26, 1999).

–   *Lease Interest in Natural Gas.* National bank's operating subsidiary may own an interest in a natural gas lease when ownership interest is equivalent to secured lending. Corporate Decision No. 98-17 (March 23, 1998). National banks may acquire an otherwise impermissible property interest in minerals, e.g., oil and gas production payments, when it is acquired in connection with the bank's express power to lend money. OCC Interpretive Letter (October 4, 1994).

–   *Lease of Personal Property for Bank's Use.* National banks may be the lessee of personal property for their own use. OCC Interpretive Letter (July 14, 1976).

–   *Lease of Public Facilities.* National banks may lease a building to a municipality as long as the lease agreement provides that the municipality will become owner of the building on expiration of the lease. 12 CFR 7.1000(d).

–   *Lease of Real Property.* National banks may lease real property that is incidental to a permissible lease of personal property, e.g., land upon which a leased manufacturing facility stands. OCC Interpretive Letter No. 770, reprinted in [1996-1997 Transfer Binder] Fed. Banking L. Rep. (CCH) ¶ 81-134 (February 10, 1997); Corporate Decision No. 98-35, 1999 OCC QJ LEXIS 189 (June 10, 1998).

–   *Leasing Bank Employees From Third Party.* National banks may lease the services of its employees from a third party as long as the board of directors continues to retain and exercise general supervision over the affairs of bank. OCC Interpretive Letter No. 431, reprinted in [1988-1989 Transfer Binder] Fed. Banking L. Rep. (CCH) 85,655 (November 5, 1987); 12 CFR 7.2010.

–   *Leasing Bank Lobby to Securities Brokers, Real Estate Brokers, Insurance Agents, and Travel Agents.* National banks may lease bank premises to unaffiliated entities and the rental payments made to the bank may be based on a percentage of gross commissions received by the tenant. 12 CFR 7.3001(a).

–   *Leasing/Selling Excess Capacity.* A national bank may lease excess monitoring capacity of its security/fire alarm system or other equipment to other financial institutions. OCC Interpretive Letter (September 17, 1987). National banks may market excess capacity on mail sorting equipment to other companies and may resell excess capacity on their long line telecommunications and data processing equipment to third parties. OCC Interpretive Letter (December 13, 1983); OCC Interpretive Letter (December 20, 1989).

- *Murabaha Financing Transactions.* A national bank may enter into net leases or installment sales of real estate to serve the home finance needs of its customers, who are prohibited by religious principles from paying interest and therefore from obtaining traditional mortgages. OCC Interpretive Letter No. 806, reprinted in [1997-1998 Transfer Binder] Fed. Banking L. Rep. (CCH) ¶81,253 (October 17, 1997); OCC Interpretive Letter No. 867 (June 1, 1999).

- *Noncontrolling Investment in Trust to Purchase, Own, Lease Aircraft.* Noncontrolling investment in a trust established to purchase, own, and lease commercial aircraft is permissible, however, because of safety and soundness concerns, the bank must charge off the investment in its entirety. OCC Interpretive Letter No. 887 (April 30, 2000).

- *Purchase of Off-Lease Equipment.* A national bank may purchase from lessors and resell, as principal, off-lease equipment. Alternatively, it may act as agent for such lessors in selling the equipment. The letter finds that these activities are part of the business of banking and authorized under 12 USC 24(Seventh) , 12 USC 24(Tenth), and 12 CFR 23. OCC Interpretive Letter No. 953 (December 4, 2002).

- *Real Estate Leasing.* A national bank's financial subsidiary proposed to engage in real estate leasing of the type that the Board of Governors of the Federal Reserve System has determined to be permissible in section 225.28(b)(3) of Regulation Y. The financial subsidiary also proposed to become a general partner of a limited partnership that would also engage in real estate leasing permitted by Regulation Y. Financial Subsidiary Filing (December 6, 2001).

Lending

- **Lending, in General.** A national bank and its operating subsidiaries may make, purchase, sell, service, or warehouse house loans or other extensions of credit for its own or another's account, including consumer loans, credit card loans, commercial loans, residential mortgage loans, commercial mortgage loans, and standby letters of credit. 12 USC 24(Seventh), 371; 12 CFR 5.34. A national bank's broad authority to lend and extend credit includes, but is not limited to, the following activities:

  - *Abundance of Caution Exception in Real Estate Appraisal.* In order to use abundance of caution exception in real estate appraisal regulation, 12 CFR 34.43(a) (2), borrower's ability to repay must be well supported by income or collateral other than real estate. Reaffirms position in OCC Interpretive Letter No. 569 that indirect real estate lending, e.g., taking as collateral promissory notes that are secured by real estate, is subject to the appraisal regulation. OCC Interpretive Letter No. 1107 (December 4, 2008).

- *Adjustable Rate Mortgages (ARM)*. National banks may make, sell, purchase, participate in or otherwise deal in ARM loans without regard to state limitations. 12 CFR 34.21 (a).

- *Advances Necessary to Preserve Business Acquired to Secure DPC*. National banks can make necessary advances to run a business and thereby preserve its going concern value when the business is acquired to secure or collect debt previously contracted (DPC). 12 CFR 34.86; OCC Interpretive Letter No. 576, reprinted in [1991-1992 Transfer Binder] Fed. Banking L. Rep. (CCH) 83,346 (March 27, 1992); OCC Interpretive Letter No. 12, reprinted in [1978-1979 Transfer Binder] Fed. Banking L. Rep. (CCH) 85,087 (December 7, 1977).

- *Agricultural Loans*. A national bank may offer agricultural loans with payments that vary based on changes in commodity prices. The proposed activities are permissible as incidental to an existing agricultural lending business. The bank first must satisfy itself concerning possible application of commodity laws to the program and must also establish to the satisfaction of the supervisory office that the bank has an appropriate risk measurement and management process. OCC Interpretive letter No. 1019 (February 10, 2005).

- *Appraisal Services*. National banks may perform real estate appraisals in connection with both their loans and loans made by other financial institutions. OCC Interpretive Letter No. 467, reprinted in [1988-1989 Transfer Binder] Fed. Banking L. Rep. (CCH) 85,646 (January 24, 1989). National bank operating subsidiaries may perform real estate appraisals for general customers, even if no bank loan is involved, pursuant to the excess capacity theory, provided that the activity constitutes no more than 10 percent of the subsidiary's business. National banks may perform appraisals for the occasional customer who requests one even though there is no associated loan transaction. Corporate Decision No. 98-25, 1999 OCC QJ LEXIS 22 (April 1, 1998); 12 CFR 34.45(a).

- *Balloon Loans*. National banks may make either conventional or repurchase balloon loans secured by personal property and real property. OCC Interpretive Letter No. 364, reprinted in [1985-1987 Transfer Binder] Fed. Banking L. Rep. (CCH) 85,534 (July 9, 1986). National banks may make fixed rate, balloon, demand, or non-regularly amortized residential mortgage loans without regard to state law to the contrary. OCC Interpretive Letter No. 38-01, 1992 WL 486907 (September 30, 1992).

- *Banker's Acceptances (i.e., commitments by financial institutions to honor drafts of customer at a future date, usually not in excess of nine months)*. National banks may issue banker's acceptances. A national bank is not limited in the character of acceptances that it may make in financing credit transactions. Accepting bank may create, buy, and sell acceptances created by any bank in a transaction with any party in any denomination, and a nonaccepting bank may purchase an acceptance of any denomination for resale to any party, including fractional interests, provided that the rights conveyed are at least equivalent to those provided in the underlying documents. 12 CFR. 7.1007.

- *Bridge Loans.* A national bank's operating subsidiary may form partnerships with the affiliate of an investment bank to make short-term bridge loans and provide advice concerning such bridge loans. OCC Interpretive Letter No. 411, reprinted in [1988-1989 Transfer Binder] Fed. Banking L. Rep. 85,635 (January 20, 1988); OCC Interpretive Letter No. 516, reprinted in [1990-1991 Transfer Binder] Fed. Banking L. Rep. (CCH) 83,220 (July 12, 1990).

- *Bridge Loans for Infrastructure Construction.* A national bank's subsidiary community development corporation may provide bridge loans to low- and moderate-income individuals and individuals living in low- and moderate-income areas to finance the installation of water and sewer infrastructure improvements. Approval of Bank's Self-Certification (December 27, 2004).

- *Combination of Church Loans Under the Direct Benefit Test Where Controlling Trust Beneficiaries Are Identical.* A national bank with four outstanding loans to four separate local churches proposed to lend additional funds to a fifth church. Because the proceeds of loans made to the local churches are used for transactions which are controlled by trusts having an identical beneficiary (the parent church), and this beneficiary is entitled to the ultimate benefit of those transactions, the loans should be combined and attributed to the beneficiary. OCC Interpretive Letter No. 925 (April 12, 2001).

- *Construction Loans to Unaffiliated Lenders.* A national bank may establish a wholly owned operating subsidiary to provide a number of real estate construction loan services to unaffiliated lenders. This was the first approval of banks providing many of these services, which banks provide for themselves, to other parties. Corporate Decision No. 2001-27 (September 13, 2001).

- *Credit Analysis for Third Parties.* National banks may perform credit analysis for third parties. OCC Interpretive Letter (October 11, 1983).

- *Credit Card Banking.* National banks may perform a variety of activities related to credit cards, including issuing credit cards, handling credit applications for other card issuers, operating a card loss notification service, and credit verification services over point of service (POS) terminals. OCC Interpretive Letter (November 14, 1980); OCC Interpretive Letter (January 25, 1979); OCC Interpretive Letter (September 18, 1975); OCC Interpretive Letter (November 14, 1974).

- *Daily Netting Requirement.* A national bank that is a member of a centralized clearing facility that requires daily netting of obligations may aggregate the daily net obligation amounts in order to determine compliance with the legal lending limit, provided that the bank excludes those days for which the net obligation amount is an amount payable by the bank. OCC Interpretive Letter No. 1088 (September 11, 2007).

– *Debt Cancellation Contracts.* For purposes of 12 CFR 37, the OCC views a national bank's extension of credit in connection with an automobile loan with a guaranteed automobile protection (GAP) feature as a single product, and does not contemplate any separate product relating to financing for the GAP feature. OCC Interpretive Letter No. 1028 (May 9, 2005).

Debt Cancellation Contracts. GAP (guaranteed automobile protection) Addendums sold by a national bank to borrowers in connection with the bank's motor vehicle loans, in connection with a GAP program administered by a third party, are debt cancellation contracts subject to 12 CFR 37. OCC Interpretive Letter No. 1032 (June 16, 2005).

– *Debt Collection.* National banks may collect delinquent loans on behalf of other lenders, may provide billing services for doctors, hospitals, or other service providers and may act as an agent in the warehousing and servicing of other loans. OCC Interpretive Letter (August 27, 1985).

– *Debt for Equity Swaps.* National banks may enter into swaps of rescheduled foreign government loans through a series of interrelated transactions and hold the equity received to extinguish the debt pursuant to the national bank's DPC authority. Similarly, national banks may exchange nonperforming or rescheduled debt acquired DPC for equity in unaffiliated companies. Letter from Ralph E. Sharpe, Deputy Comptroller Multinational banking, dated September 25, 1996; Letter from Ralph E. Sharpe, Deputy Comptroller Multinational banking, dated February 25, 1997; Letter from Ralph E. Sharpe, Deputy Comptroller Multinational banking, dated March 25, 1997; OCC Interpretive Letter No. 643, reprinted in [1994 Transfer Binder] Fed. Banking L. Rep. (CCH) 83,551 (July 1, 1992); OCC Interpretive Letter No. 511, reprinted in [1990-1991 Transfer Binder] Fed. Banking L. Rep. (CCH) (July 20, 1990).

– *Debtor Bank Located in State of Its Main Office for UCC Purposes.* As a general matter, under revised Article 9 of the Uniform Commercial Code, the location of the debtor determines which state's law governs perfection of a security interest. Section 9-307 determines the location of debtors for choice of law purposes. For purposes of this section, a debtor national bank is located in the state in which its main office is located. OCC Interpretive Letter No. 913 (August 5, 2001).

– *Direct Deposit Advance Program.* A direct deposit advance program, characterized as a program of advances, pursuant to a written agreement with the customer, made to a participating deposit account in defined increments, with a fixed finance charge per increment, and limited to a portion of a customer's monthly direct deposit deposits up to a maximum balance, to be repaid upon crediting of subsequent direct deposits, or charged in full to the customer's account if not repaid within a specified time frame, constitutes open-end consumer credit for purposes of the Truth in Lending Act and Regulation Z. OCC Interpretive Letter (April 11, 2001), publication pending.

– *Disbursing Agent.* National banks may act as disbursing agent for loans made by another bank. OCC Interpretive Letter (October 18, 1974).

– *Economic Development Loans to Native Americans.* National banks may make loans to certain authorized Native American organizations, with at least 20 percent of the loans guaranteed, without being subject to restrictions of other statutes regarding loan to value ratios, maturity, security, priority of lien or percentage of assets that may be invested. 25 USC 1489.

– *Escrow Services.* National banks may provide escrow services. OCC Interpretive Letter (May 6, 1968).

– *Exchange of Interest in Real Property Acquired in Satisfaction of a Debt Previously Contracted for Interest in an Entity That Would Dispose of the Real Property.* A national bank may exchange an interest in real property acquired in satisfaction of a debt previously contracted for an interest in an entity that would dispose of the real property. Prior to making the exchange, 1) the bank's directors must determine that the exchange is in the best interests of the bank and would improve the ability of the bank to recover, or otherwise limit, its loan loss, and 2) the bank must notify its supervisory office, in writing, of the proposed exchange and receive written notification of supervisory no-objection. OCC Interpretive Letter No. 1118 (July 2, 2009).

– *Exportation of Interest Rates.* 12 USC 85, including "most favored lender" provision, applies to operating subsidiaries in the same manner and to the same extent that it applies to the parent national bank. OCC Interpretive Letters No. 968 (February 12, 2003) and 974 (July 21, 2003).

– *Financing Through Interest in LLC.* A national bank may hold an interest in a limited liability company structured to be substantially equivalent to an extension of credit, to finance an alternative energy project. The LLC would, in turn, hold interests in real estate in connection with its business. The proposed structure facilitates the provision of financing by permitting the bank to receive federal tax credits and reducing the cost of financing. OCC Interpretive Letter No. 1048 (December 12, 2005).

– *Flood Hazard Determinations.* National banks may provide mortgage lenders with flood hazard determination services. Corporate Decision No. 97-79, (July 11, 1997).

– *Home Equity Lines of Credit.* In a national bank's securitization of its own home equity lines of credit (HELOC), the bank may hold the securitized HELOC notes as Type V securities, the usual 25 percent prudential limit is not intended to apply under the specific facts and circumstances represented, and retention of the subordinated interest is permissible under 12 USC 24 (Seventh). The conclusions are subject to various safety and soundness requirements. The appropriate risk-based capital treatment is the risk-based capital charge for the underlying HELOC. OCC Interpretive Letter No. 1035 (July 21, 2005).

– *Insider Loans.* A national bank violates Regulation O if an insider loan is either: (i) preferential or (ii) involves more than the normal risk of repayment or presents other unfavorable features. To the extent that earlier OCC staff opinions have suggested otherwise, they are overruled. Earlier staff opinions concluded that both requirements (i) and (ii) must be met in order to violate Regulation O. OCC Interpretive Letter No. 1024 (March 21, 2005).

– *Investment in a Firm Engaged in Check Cashing and Payday Lending.* A national bank may make a noncontrolling investment in a firm engaged in check cashing and payday lending activities where the bank would use the firm to educate consumers about traditional banking services, alternatives to payday loans, and the limited proper use of such loans, would cause the firm to provide enhanced disclosures about payday loans, including information about the cost of multiple rollovers, would limit the use of payday loans, such as by imposing annual limits and limits on rollovers, and would assess lower fees for rollover transactions. The firm's check cashing operations also were intended to be used as a vehicle to transition customers into more traditional bank products such as savings accounts. Noncontrolling Investment Notification (March 14, 2000).

– *Lending Limits.* Lending limits in 12 USC 84 and the public welfare investments limits of 12 USC 24(11) are separate and independent of each other. OCC Interpretive Letter No. 1076 (November 14, 2006).

– *Lending Limit Exception for Marketable Staples.* The lending limit exception for marketable staples secured by warehouse receipts, 12 USC 84(c)(3) and 12 CFR 32.3(b)(1)(iv)(B), does not apply if the borrower registers the warehouse receipts with an independent third party but retains control of the staples. The borrower was the owner of the elevator in which the staples were stored. OCC Interpretive Letter No. 895 (June 22, 2000).

– *Lending Limit for Bank Premises.* A national bank may make a loan to an unrelated borrower that exceeds the bank's lending limit when the borrower will use the proceeds to construct a new premises building for the bank. The limitations on loans and investments for bank premises contained in 12 USC 371d take precedence over the general lending limits in 12 USC 84. OCC Interpretive Letter No. 950 (December 18, 2002).

– *Lending Limit for Loans Guaranteed by the Illinois Farm Development Authority.* Loans guaranteed by the Illinois Farm Development Authority (IFDA) qualify for the lending limit exception contained in 12 CFR 2.3(c)(5) because of an Illinois Attorney General opinion stating that IFDA loan guarantees are backed by the full faith and credit of the State of Illinois. OCC Interpretive Letter No. 889 (April 24, 2000).

- *Lending Limit for Loans to Leasing Companies.* Letter concludes that the leasing exception at 12 CFR 32.3(c)(10) can apply when the proceeds of the loan to the leasing company are not used directly to purchase the assets to be leased but rather are used to reimburse the leasing company for the past purchase of such assets. OCC Interpretive Letter No. 955 (January 31, 2003).

- *Lending Limit for Loans to Related Entities.* Letter addresses the application of the various loan combination/attribution rules at 12 CFR 32.5 to loans to several related entities. The letter also addresses the issue of how to treat the gross income from a subchapter S corporation that is reported as part of the shareholder's adjusted gross income on his or her federal tax return in determining substantial financial interdependence for the purpose of 12 CFR 32.5(c)(2). OCC Interpretive Letter No.951 (January 17, 2002).

- *Lending Limit Pilot Program.* Two loans by the same bank to the same borrower, one having a first lien and the other having a second lien on the same residential real estate, qualify for the OCC's special lending limit pilot program. OCC Interpretive Letter No. 1050 (January 25, 2006).

- *Lending Limit Pilot Program.* A loan to finance land development or construction, whether secured by the real property or not, does not qualify for the lending limit pilot program in 12 CFR 32.7. OCC Interpretive Letter No. 942 (June 11, 2002).

- *Lending Limit Relief.* A lending bank may obtain relief from the lending limit upon the sale of loan participations provided the participations meet certain requirements under 12 CFR 32.2(k)(2)(vi). The lending limit participation rule contains no reference to applicable accounting standards and, accordingly, conformity with sale requirements under such standards is not required. OCC Interpretive Letter No. 1134 (August 2, 2011).

- *Lending Limit Wind Tower Lending.* Letter addresses the applicability of the lending limit combination rules to loans to wind tower companies that sell their output to the same power company. OCC Interpretive Letter No. 1074 (November 21, 2006).

- *Loan Agreements Providing for a Share in Profits, Income, or Earnings, or for Stock Warrants.* National banks may make loans and accept from the borrower in lieu of interest, a share of the borrower's profits, equity in the borrower, stock warrants (provided they are not exercised), or stock dividend payments. 12 CFR 7.1006; OCC Interpretive Letter (May 8, 1989).

- *Loan Attribution to One Entity Through Common Enterprise Test.* A national bank proposed to make loans to two entities (A and B) that were related through the common control of a third entity (X). A and B each pays more than 50 percent of its gross annual expenditures to the controlling entity X. Accordingly, the proposed loans to A and B would be attributed to X under 12 CFR 32.5(c)(2) and thus combined for purposes of the legal lending limit, even where X does not borrow directly from the national bank. OCC Interpretive Letter No. 938 (January 18, 2001).

- *Loan Origination and Servicing Activities.* A national bank's operating subsidiary may engage in loan origination and servicing activities, as well as commercial mortgage loan brokerage services. OCC Interpretive Letter No. 387, reprinted in [1988-1989 Transfer Binder] Fed. Banking L. Rep. (CCH) ¶ 85,611 (June 22, 1987). National bank's operating subsidiary may make, purchase, sell, service or warehouse loans, or other extensions of credit for its own or another's account, including consumer loans, credit card loans, commercial loans, residential mortgage loans, and commercial mortgage loans. 12 CFR 5.34(e)(2)(ii)(L), 34.1(b).

- *Loan Participations.* National banks may purchase participation interests in pooled loans. OCC Interpretive Letter No. 579, reprinted in [1991-1992 Transfer Binder] Fed. Banking L. Rep. (CCH) ¶ 183,349 (March 24, 1992).

- *Loan Production Offices.* National banks may establish a loan production office to solicit and originate business outside of its main office and authorized branches. 12 CFR 7.1004, 7.1005; Banking Circular No. 199, reprinted in 4 Banking L. Rep. (CCH) ¶ 45-595 (May 23, 1985).

- *Loan Repurchase Agreements.* National banks may agree to repurchase loans or other assets. OCC Interpretive Letter No. 415, reprinted in [1988-1989 Transfer Binder] Fed. Banking L. Rep. (CCH) ¶ 85,639 (February 12, 1987); 12 CFR 32.2.

- *Loans Secured by Insured, Non-Negotiable Certificates of Deposit.* Loans secured by insured, non-negotiable certificates of deposit issued by other financial institutions do not qualify for the additional lending limit for loans secured by readily marketable collateral, or for the lending limit exception for loans secured by U.S Government-guaranteed loans. OCC Interpretive Letter No. 1061 (April 28, 2006).

- *Loans Secured by Liens on Real Estate.* A national bank that wishes to acquire loans from a securitization trust, which is in process of winding down, also may acquire for a moment-in-time Debt Previously Contracted (DPC) real estate from the trust. Prior to such acquisition, the national bank must have an agreement in place to re-sell the DPC real estate immediately to a third party. OCC Interpretive Letter No. 1097 (April 3, 2008).

- *Loans to an Employee Stock Option Plan (ESOP).* A national bank, as a disqualified person who serves as trustee or service provider to an ESOP, may make qualified term loans through its commercial loan division to a company sponsoring an ESOP. Trust Interpretation No. 241, reprinted in [1989-1990 Transfer Binder] Fed. Banking L. Rep. (CCH) 183,082 (November 14, 1989).

– *Margin Loans.* National bank's operating subsidiary may make margin loans. OCC Interpretive Letter No. 326, reprinted in [1985-1987 Transfer Binder] Fed. Banking L. Rep. (CCH) ¶ 85,496 (January 17, 1985).

– *Mortgage Document Custodian.* National banks may act as document custodians of residential mortgage loan documents for third parties without obtaining approval to exercise trust powers. 12 USC 24(Seventh).

– *Mortgage Modification and Foreclosure Avoidance Scams—Consumer Advisory.* The OCC issued a consumer advisory to help homeowners avoid scams that claim to help them save their homes, but can cause them to lose their homes and their money. The advisory describes common types of mortgage modification and foreclosure rescue scams, and offers a list of warning signs that a person or company may be perpetrating one of these scams. The advisory also gives tips for consumers to protect themselves from these scams, provides a list of resources to contact for legitimate help, including information on U.S. government loan programs and counseling resources, and reminds consumers having difficulty paying their mortgages that they should always start by contacting their lender or servicer to discuss their options. OCC Consumer Advisory 2009-1 (April 21, 2009).

– *Most Favored Lender.* Under "most favored lender" provision of 12 USC 85 and Michigan parity statute, if state-chartered banks may charge prepayment fees to the same extent as federal savings associations, then national banks may, as well. OCC Interpretive Letter No. 1004 (August 4, 2004).

– *Offshore Operating Subsidiary.* A national bank may establish an offshore operating subsidiary that will facilitate the funding of the bank's domestic mortgage lending operations. The subsidiary's books and records must be maintained in the United States and be accessible to the OCC. Conditional Approval No. 536 (June 21, 2002).

– *Officer Residence.* The executive officer residence exception in Federal Reserve Regulation O, 12 CFR 215.5(c)(2), applies to a single loan secured by a first lien on one residence. Loans secured by an unconditional takeout commitment from the Federal Home Loan Mortgage Corporation ("Freddie Mac") do not qualify for the government agency takeout exception in 12 CFR 215.4(d)(3)(i)(B). OCC Interpretive Letter No. 1009 (August 12, 2004).

– *Overdraft Fees Not Interest.* A national bank's flat fee charges to deposit customers for checks written without sufficient funds on deposit do not constitute "interest" limited by 12 USC 85. The fee is a processing fee, not compensation for an extension of credit. VideoTrax, Inc. v. NationsBank, N.A., 33 F.Supp.2d 1041 (S.D. Fla. 1998), aff'd 205 F.3d 1358 (11th Cir. 2000), cert. den. 1212 S. Ct. 66 (October 2, 2000).

– *Purchase of Open Accounts/Factoring.* A national bank may purchase open accounts as a part of the business of banking. A national bank also may purchase open accounts in connection with export transactions; the accounts should be protected by insurance, such as that provided by the Foreign Credit Insurance Association and the Export-Import Bank. 12 CFR 7.1020.

- *Real Estate Tax and Management Services.* National banks can establish operating subsidiaries to hold an interest in a joint venture engaged in real estate tax reporting and management services in connection with certain loans made by the bank or its lending affiliates. Conditional Approval No. 317 (July 19, 1999).

- *Regulation O.* If loans that were made before the borrower became an executive officer of the bank exceed the amounts permitted by Regulation O, they are grandfathered and do not violate Regulation O. However, no new loans may be made until loan balances are brought within Regulation O's limits. OCC Interpretive Letter No. 1096 (March 20, 2008).

- *Reverse Mortgage—Consumer Advisory.* The OCC issued a consumer advisory to help consumers better understand reverse mortgages. The information developed for consumers discusses basic facts about reverse mortgages, which are complex, home-secured loans. The advisory provides basic "rules of thumb" for consumers who are considering a reverse mortgage—the advisory urges consumers to 1) investigate other alternatives in addition to reverse mortgages, 2) remember that reverse mortgages generally make more sense the longer the consumer remains in the home, and 3) be wary of anyone trying to sell other products along with a reverse mortgage. The OCC urges consumers to consult with a qualified, independent housing counselor before entering into a reverse mortgage. OCC Consumer Advisory 2009-2 (September 24, 2009).

- *Same Source of Repayment.* On the specific facts presented, the same source of repayment test in 12 CFR 32.5(c)(1) does not result in the combination of loans to members of the Lower Sioux Indian Community with loans to other members or with a loan to the Community, itself. OCC Interpretive Letter No. 979 (December 18, 2003).

- *Service Fees for Loan Payoff Information.* A national bank and its operating subsidiaries may charge expedited service fees for loan payoff information. OCC Interpretive Letter No. 1069 (August 21, 2006).

- *Share of Profits as Part of Interest.* A national bank may: 1) take a share of borrower's profits as part of interest on loans, 12 CFR 7.1006; 2) negotiate percentage of profits bank will take; and 3) compensate borrower for originating loans by providing borrower with office space and paying borrower's expenses, 12 CFR 7.1004(a). OCC Interpretive Letter No. 956 (January 31, 2003).

- *Shared Appreciation Mortgage Loans.* National banks may make shared appreciation mortgage loans to developers for the conversion of residential property into condominium units and receive a fixed amount or percentage of the sales price of each unit sold as a share of the profit, income, and earnings. National banks may also finance the acquisition or improvement of real property on which the borrower will operate its business and receive a percentage of the appreciation of the business's value as interest on the loan. OCC Interpretive Letter No. 244, reprinted in [1983-1984 Transfer Binder] Fed. Banking L. Rep. (CCH) 185,408 (January 26, 1982); 12 CFR 7.1006.

– *Title Abstracting Services*. A national bank and its subsidiaries may provide title abstracting services for the parent bank, for unaffiliated lenders, and for the occasional customer who requests the service even if no associated loan transaction exists. 12 USC 24(Seventh); Corporate Decision No. 98-26, 1999 OCC QJ LEXIS 22 (April 21, 1998).

– *Volumetric Production Payment Loan Transaction*. A volumetric production payment financing transaction is a permissible extension of credit. Before extending credit, the bank must notify its EIC, in writing, of the proposed activities and must receive written notification of the EIC's supervisory no-objection. OCC Interpretive Letter No. 1117 (May 19, 2009).

Other Activities

- **Banking Services for State Lottery Manager**. A national bank is not prohibited from taking deposits from, and providing ordinary banking services to, a state lottery or its private manager under 12 USC 25a. Such services are expressly authorized by subsection (d). OCC Interpretive Letter No. 1085 (March 8, 2007).

- **Bank-Owned Variable Life Insurance Invested in Equity Securities**. In certain circumstances, bank-owned variable life insurance may be invested in equity securities in connection with employee compensation and benefit plans. Such insurance can be used in connection with defined contribution plans but not defined benefit plans. OCC Interpretive Letter No. 926 (September 7, 2001).

- **Borrow Money and Pledge Assets**. National banks have authority to borrow money and may pledge assets to secure their borrowings. 12 USC 24(Seventh); OCC Interpretive Letter (August 6, 1965).

- **Certificates of Deposit Purchase and Sale of Participation**. A national bank may offer participation interests in certificates of deposit purchased as agent from third parties on behalf of a number of the bank's depositors. OCC Interpretive Letter No. 385, reprinted in [1988-1989 Transfer Binder] Fed. Banking L. Rep. (CCH) 85-609 (June 19, 1987).

- **Coin and Bullion**. National bank may dispose of coins discovered in its vaults at fair market value, pursuant to 12 USC 24(Seventh) and OCC Banking Circular 58 (Rev)., even though that may exceed the value of the metallic content or the face value. Since coins were acquired in the course of normal banking operations, disposal at fair market value does not constitute impermissible speculation. OCC Interpretive Letter No. 975 (October 14, 2003).

- **Coins, Buying and Selling**. National banks may buy and sell privately minted commemorative coins, as an extension of their authority to exchange "coin or bullion." 12 USC 24(Seventh).

- **Commercial Paper Placement**. National banks, as agents, may privately place third-party commercial paper. Securities Industry Assoc. v. Board of Governors of Federal Reserve System, 807 F.2d 1052 (D.C. Cir. 1986), cert. denied, 483 U.S. 1005 (1987).

- **Consumer Access/Discount Card Program**. National banks may operate a consumer access/discount card program. OCC Interpretive Letter No. 678, reprinted in [1994-1995 Transfer Binder] Fed. Banking L. Rep. (CCH) ¶ 83,626 (July 6, 1995).

- **Courier/Messenger Services**. A national bank may establish and operate a messenger service to transport items relevant to the national bank's transactions with its customers, including courier services between financial institutions. 12 CFR 7.1012. However, national banks must receive approval from the OCC to establish a branch if the messenger service constitutes a branching function within the meaning of 12 USC 36(j). National bank may use a messenger service established and operated by a third party to pick up from and deliver to its customers items that relate to a branching function without regard to the branching limitations of 12 USC 36. National banks may also provide limited security guard escort service. OCC Interpretive Letter (October 5, 1983).

- **Debt Cancellation and Debt Suspension Agreements**. National banks may offer debt cancellation agreements providing for discharge of and obligation upon the death or disability of a borrower. 12 CFR 7.1013. Similarly, national banks may offer credit card debt suspension agreements providing for suspension of a borrower's repayment obligations in the event of the borrower's disability or unemployment. OCC Interpretive Letter No. 827, reprinted in [1997-1998 Transfer Binder] Fed. Banking L. Rep. (CCH) ¶ 81-276 (April 3, 1998).

- **Disposal of Real Property Acquired for Debts Previously Contracted (DPC)**. National banks may dispose of DPC real estate through a transfer to the banks' community development corporation (CDC) subsidiary. The CDC may hold the property pursuant to 12 USC 24(Eleventh). National banks must comply with the requirements in 12 USC 24 to dispose of such real estate. OCC Interpretive Letter No. 1131 (April 15, 2011).

- **Diversity Jurisdiction**. The U.S. Court of Appeals for the Fifth Circuit, affirming the court below, held that, under 28 USC 1348, the statute governing the citizenship of national banks for the purpose of federal court diversity jurisdiction, a national bank is not "located" in every state in which it has a branch office. Instead, it is a citizen only of the states of its principal place of business and, if different, the state identified in its articles of association. Horton v. Bank One, N.A., 387 F.3d 426 (5th Cir., October 5, 2004).

- **Diversity Jurisdiction**. Denying a petition for rehearing and rehearing en banc on January 28, 2005, the Fourth Circuit Court of Appeals let stand its November 1, 2004 opinion in which a divided panel of the court concluded that a national bank is a citizen of each state in which it has a branch office. In the decision, the panel majority construed the text of 28 USC 1348 (which states that national banks are "deemed citizens of the States in which they are respectively located") to unambiguously provide that national banks are citizens of each state where they have a significant permanent presence. The Fourth Circuit's decision is in conflict with decisions of the Fifth and Seventh Circuits construing the same language. Wachovia Bank v. Schmidt, 388 F.3d 414 (4th Cir. 2004). Citing the circuit split created by the decision in Wachovia v. Schmidt, the plaintiff in Horton v. Bank One, N.A., filed a petition for certiorari with the Supreme Court seeking review of the Fifth Circuit's decision holding, in agreement with the Seventh Circuit, that a national bank is a citizen of at most two states, the state where its main office is located and the state where it has its principal place of business. Although Bank One prevailed in the Court of Appeals, it has asked the Supreme Court to grant the petition for certiorari to resolve the circuit split. Horton v. Bank One, N.A., 387 F.3d 426 (5th Cir. 2004).

- **Dividends—Treatment of the Service Cost on Innovative Capital Instrument**. "Service costs" paid on an innovative capital instrument by a operating subsidiary to third party investors constitute a dividend for the purposes of 12 USC 60. However, to avoid double counting of the service costs, the bank may adjust its net income for distributions on innovative capital instruments that are treated as dividends. OCC Interpretive Letter No. 1067 (February 28, 2006).

- **Donation of Fundraising Item**. A national bank may donate an item for a community fundraising raffle without violating the lottery prohibition of 12 USC 25a if the bank was identified as the donor of the item in publicity issued by the raffle sponsors, if the publicity was not displayed on bank premises. OCC Interpretive Letter 900 (June 19, 2000).

- **Employee Relocation Services**. Letter provides that an operating subsidiary of a national bank may acquire, for a short period of time and subject to conditions requiring retransfer, title to the relocating employees' residential real estate as incidental to the package of relocation services offered by the subsidiary. OCC Interpretive Letter 966 (May 12, 2003).

- **Escrow Activities**. A national bank's proposed escrow activities are part of the business of banking pursuant to 12 USC 24(Seventh) and 12 CFR 7.5001 & 7.5002. OCC Interpretive Letter No. 1041 (September 28, 2005).

- **Federal Diversity Jurisdiction**. On January 17, 2006, the Supreme Court unanimously held that for purposes of diversity jurisdiction, a national bank is a citizen of the one state where it maintains its main office as set forth in the bank's articles of association. The Court's decision reversed a Fourth Circuit decision holding that a national bank is a citizen of every state in which it maintains a branch office or potentially any other physical presence. Wachovia Bank, Nat. Ass'n v. Schmidt, U.S. (2006), 126 S.Ct. 941, reversing 388 F.3d 414 (4th Cir. 2004). See Horton v. Bank One, N.A., 387 F.3d 426 (5th Cir. 2004), cert. denied U.S. (January 23, 2006).

- **Foreign Investment Company Owning National Bank**. A foreign-based global investment management company, which is not a bank holding company, is not covered by the International Banking Act, and is not subject to comprehensive consolidated supervision, may own a national bank, provided: the OCC would have access to all books and records of the bank's parents that concern the bank; through a written binding agreement the parent will provide capital maintenance and liquidity support to the bank; the bank will not engage in covered transactions with foreign affiliates unless the bank notifies the OCC in advance and maintains documentation on the transaction and has available for OCC review financial information on the affiliate; all transactions between the bank and any affiliate will be conducted subject to 12 USC 371c, 371c-1 or other applicable federal law; the bank will adopt and implement policies, procedures and internal controls reasonably designed to encompass anti-money laundering efforts; and the parent must maintain a designated agent in the United States. Conditional Approval No. 425 (November 8, 2000).

- **Golden Parachute Payments**. A U.S. district court granted the OCC and FDIC summary judgment in a challenge to the agencies' denial of a national bank's request for permission to make a severance payment and annual split dollar insurance premium payments to a terminated senior executive officer. The former executive officer challenged the interpretation of the golden parachute statute and regulations on which the agencies based their findings that the payments at issue were golden parachute payments and that reasonable grounds existed on which to base a denial. The court found that the agencies' interpretation and implementation of the law were reasonable. Knyal v. OCC, FDIC, No. C 02-2851 PJH (N.D. Cal., November 25, 2003).

- **Indicia of Ownership of Real Property**. A national bank operating subsidiary may acquire and hold certain indicia of ownership of real estate when incidental to the package of relocation services offered by that subsidiary. There are several restrictions and conditions: the subsidiary must use a nominee to hold legal title; the subsidiary may not use or enjoy the benefit of the property; the subsidiary may not manage the property; and the subsidiary must dispose of the indicia within 90 days. OCC Interpretive Letter No. 966 (May 12, 2003).

- **Interest on Lawyers Trust Account Board/NOW Accounts**. Interest-bearing negotiable order of withdrawal ("NOW") accounts may be established at national banks for the purpose of receiving and holding qualified trust funds deposited under the Pennsylvania Supreme Court's Interest on Trust Account Program for the Minor Judiciary. OCC Interpretive Letter No. 1017 (January 28, 2005).

- **Internal Bank Financing Operations Offshore**. A national bank may form an operating subsidiary in the Cayman Islands to engage in internal bank financial operations, provided the OCC would have access to all books and records, no activities were conducted offshore, and the subsidiary would be subject to OCC examination, supervision, and regulation. Conditional Approval No. 413 (September 22, 2000).

- **Lease of Personal Property to an Affiliate Under 12 CFR Part 23.** When a bank acts as the lessor of personal property and the lease is subject to section 23A of the Federal Reserve Act and Federal Reserve Regulation W, the value of the transaction, i.e., the amount of the covered transaction, is the book value of the leased property. The leased property may serve as collateral for purposes of section 23A and Regulation W. OCC Interpretive Letter No. 1114 (April 9, 2009).

- **Messenger Service.** A national bank may operate a messenger service that will provide pickup and delivery of cash, checks, and other financial items for nonfinancial institution businesses having no deposit relationship with the bank. Items will be transported between facilities of such businesses, and between such businesses and their financial institutions. Corporate Decision No. 2003-9 (June 25, 2003).

- **"On Us" Check Cashing Fees.** National banks may charge a nonaccountholder a convenience fee for using a bank teller to cash an "on us" check. An "on us" check is a check drawn on the bank by one of the bank's customers. As noted in these letters, this fee is essentially compensating the bank for making cash immediately available to the payee; otherwise, the payee would have to wait for the check to clear through the payment system. These fees are authorized under 12 USC 24(Seventh) and 12 CFR 7.4002(a). OCC Interpretive Letters No. 932, 933 (August 17, 2001) and 934 (August 20, 2001).

- **Order of Check Posting.** A national bank's decision concerning the order of posting checks presented for payment is a pricing decision authorized by 12 USC 24(Seventh) and 12 CFR 7.4002. This would permit the bank to pay the largest check first from an account in a given 24-hour cycle. OCC Interpretive Letter No. 916 (May 22, 2001).

- **Payment Processor Guidance.** OCC supervisory guidance to national banks discussing due diligence, underwriting, and monitoring of entities that process payments for telemarketers and other merchant clients, in order to control strategic, credit, transaction, reputation, and compliance risks, including risks associated with customer complaints, returned items, and potential unfair or deceptive acts or practices. OCC Bulletin 2008-12, "Payment Processors: Risk Management Guidance" (April 24, 2008).

- **Postal Services.** National banks may maintain, operate, and receive income from postal substations on banking premises, pursuant to U.S. Postal Service regulations. National banks may advertise, develop, and extend the services of the substation to attract customers. The services performed at the substations must be permitted by the U.S. Postal Service and may include meter stamping of letters and packages, and the sale of related insurance. National banks must keep the books and records of the substations, which are subject to inspection by the U.S. Postal Service, separate from those of other banking operations. 12 CFR 7.1010; 39 CFR 241.2. National banks may sell stamp collecting kits and stamps for collection in accordance with post office regulations, but need to be full-fledged postal stations to do this. OCC Interpretive Letter (December 1975).

- **Printing Service**. A national bank may engage in the printing of checks, drafts, loan payment coupons, and similar documents for use in the national bank's business; engage in printing services that facilitate the general operation of the bank as a business enterprise, such as the printing of internal personnel forms; and provide printing services for affiliated banks. 12 USC 24(Seventh); OCC Interpretive Letter No. 811, reprinted in [1997-1998 Transfer Binder] Fed. Banking L. Rep. (CCH) ¶ 81,259 (December 18, 1997).

- **Purchasing and Selling Transferable State Tax Credits**. A national bank is authorized under 12 USC 24(Seventh) to purchase and resell, as principal, transferable state tax credits. This is a financial intermediary activity and therefore part of the business of banking. OCC Interpretive Letter No. 948 (October 23, 2002).

- **"Qualified Intermediary" for Reverse Like-Kind Exchanges**. A national bank's operating subsidiary, through limited liability corporation subsidiaries, may act as a "qualified intermediary" for investors interested in consummating tax-deferred "reverse like-kind exchanges" of real properties. Internal Revenue Code, 26 USC 1031, permits like-kind exchanges, which allow investors to exchange certain investment property, including real property, for other investment property, subject to certain limitations. In a reverse like-kind exchange, investors identify and acquire replacement properties before disposing of relinquished properties. As a qualified intermediary, the operating subsidiary is an independent party that facilitates the process by acquiring an interest in the replacement real property without acquiring full legal title in the property, and by providing proper documentation to preserve the integrity of the transaction for IRS purposes. Corporate Decision No. 2001-30 (October 10, 2001).

- **Real Estate Construction Services**. A national bank may establish a wholly owned operating subsidiary to furnish administrative, management, and consulting services to unaffiliated real estate construction lenders and investors. The services may include project feasibility, cost, contract, environmental and seismic reviews; appraisals; loan document preparation; collateral and construction phase completion monitoring; syndicated loan lead agent tasks; and lender training on construction loan administration. Corporate Decision No. 2001-27 (September 13, 2001).

- **Reverse Like-Kind Exchange Services**. A national bank may serve as exchange accommodation titleholder for customers engaging in reverse like-kind exchange transactions. As part of this service, the bank may acquire a severely circumscribed, indirect interest in real estate being exchanged. Conditional Approval No. 706 (October 6, 2005).

- **Support Services, in General**. National banks may act as agents for an individual or corporation without obtaining prior approval to exercise trust powers if the duties are nondiscretionary and purely ministerial in nature. The following are examples of these services:

- *Agent for Deposit Placement*. A national bank may place deposits as agent for its customers with other financial institutions pursuant to 12 USC 24(Seventh). Investments Securities Letter No. 32, reprinted in [1989-1990 Transfer Binder] Fed. Banking L. Rep. (CCH) ¶ 83,038 (December 2, 1988); OCC Interpretive Letter No. 778, reprinted in [1997 Transfer Binder] Fed. Banking L. Rep. (CCH) ¶ 81,205 (March 20, 1997) (placing deposits at foreign banks on behalf of customers on an agency basis and offering this service over the Internet).

- *Agent for Purchasing or Selling Government Securities*. National banks may act as agents in the purchase and sale of government securities. 12 CFR 13.

- *Agent for Purchasing or Selling Real Estate Limited Partnership Interests*. National banks may act as agent in the purchase and sale of financial investment instruments, such as real estate limited partnership interests. OCC Interpretive Letter No. 420, reprinted in [1988-1989 Transfer Binder] Fed. Banking L. Rep. (CCH) ¶ 85,644 (March 14, 1988).

- *Agent of Service of Process*. National banks subsidiary may act as agent for service of process on behalf of bank and/or its affiliates as furnishing of services of this nature for a bank or its affiliates is part of or incidental to the business of banking. Corporate Decision No. 97-14, (March 4, 1997).

- **Tax-Related Services**. National banks may assist customers in preparing tax returns directly or through subsidiaries for any type of customer. 12 USC 4(Seventh); 12 CFR 7.1008.

- **Travel Services and Foreign Exchange Activities**. National banks may sell traveler's checks and foreign currency, make travel-related loans, issue letters of credit and provide free travel information. National banks also may assist customers in placing orders for tickets with a travel agency and, in general, lease excess office space to a travel agency. OCC Interpretive Letter No. 437, reprinted in [1988-1989 Transfer Binder] Fed. Banking L. Rep. (CCH) ¶ 85,611 (July 27, 1988); OCC Interpretive Letter No. 342, reprinted in [1985-1987 Transfer Binder] Fed. Banking L. Rep. (CCH) ¶ 85, 644 (May 22, 1985).

- **Trucking Company, Credit and Other Services**. National banks may offer credit, fleet management and tracking, inventory control, and accounting services to trucking companies. OCC Interpretive Letter (August 15, 1983).

Payment Services

- **Cash Management**. National banks may provide cash management services. OCC Interpretive Letter No. 756, reprinted in [1996-1997 Transfer Binder] Fed. Banking L. Rep. (CCH) 181-120 (November 5, 1996.)

- **Cash Management Computer Software**. National banks or bank operating subsidiaries may invest in a limited liability company that develops, produces, and distributes or sells cash management software. OCC Interpretive Letter No. 677, reprinted in [1994-1995 Transfer Binder] Fed. Banking L. Rep. (CCH) 183-625 (June 28, 1995); OCC Interpretive Letter No. 756, reprinted in [1996-1997 Transfer Binder] Fed. Banking L. Rep. (CCH) 181-120 (November 5, 1996); OCC Interpretive Letter No. 284, reprinted in [1983-1984 Transfer Binder] Fed. Banking L. Rep. (CCH) 85,448 (March 26, 1984).

- **Cashiers' Checks, Money Orders, Savings Bonds, and Travelers Checks**. National banks may issue, collect, and process cashiers' checks and money orders. National banks may also sell savings bonds and travelers checks. 12 USC 24(Seventh).

- **Check Cashing and Processing**. National banks may cash and process checks, and may provide check and credit card verification services. 12 USC 24(Seventh).

- **Check Certification**. National banks may certify checks, provided the person, firm, or corporation drawing the check has sufficient funds on deposit to cover it. 12 USC 501. National banks may guarantee drafts drawn against a bank customer. OCC Interpretive Letter (October 29, 1968).

- **Letters of Credit**. National banks may issue and commit to issue letters of credit and other independent undertakings within the scope of the applicable laws or rules of practice recognized by law. Under such letters of credit and other independent undertakings, the bank's obligation to honor depends upon the presentation of specified documents and not upon nondocumentary conditions or resolution of questions of fact or law at issue between the account party and the beneficiary. A national bank may also confirm or otherwise undertake to honor or purchase specified documents upon their presentation under another person's independent undertaking within the scope of such laws or rules.

Fiduciary Activities

- **Fiduciary Activity, in General**. National banks with fiduciary powers (which may be granted at the time of chartering or subsequently on application to the OCC) are subject to federal rules that define fiduciary standards and authorize national banks to operate in the same capacities as fiduciaries are permitted to operate in the states where the bank conducts its trust activities. 12 USC 92a and 12 CFR 9. National banks also may operate as limited purpose trust banks and need not engage in all banking functions. Fiduciary activities include:

  - *Collective Investment Funds*. A national bank's model-driven funds, established pursuant to 12 CFR 9.18, may allocate costs to individual participants being admitted to or withdrawing from such funds in the same manner and to the same extent as section 9.18 index funds. OCC Interpretive Letter No. 919 (November 9, 2001).

– *Collective Investment Trust Admissions and Withdrawals.* Annual admissions and withdrawals are permitted where circumstances warrant under section 9.18, and therefore an exemption from section 9.18 is not required. OCC Interpretive Letter No.920 (December 6, 2001).

– *Collective Investment Trust Withdrawals.* A national bank, as trustee, may allow participant withdrawals from a collective investment fund solely at the bank's discretion, or when a participant becomes ineligible to continue as a participant in the fund. 12 CFR 9.18 does not mandate the frequency of admissions and withdrawals from collective investment funds. OCC Interpretive Letter No. 936 (May 22, 2002).

– *Collective Investment Funds (CIF)/Common Trust Funds.* National banks may invest fiduciary assets in collective investment funds. 12 CFR 9.18. National banks may charge a different management fee to CIF participants, commensurate with the amount and types of services they provide to participants. OCC Interpretive Letter No. 829, reprinted in [1997-98 Transfer Binder] Fed. Banking L. Rep. (CCH) ¶ 81,278 (April 9, 1998).

– *Custody Trust Ledger Deposit Account Program.* A national bank's custody activities with respect to the described Custody Trust Ledger Deposit Account Program are permissible, and the program's non-cash earnings credit feature is not inconsistent with safe and sound banking practices. The program provides for the deposit by broker-dealers of customer funds in accordance with SEC Rule 15c3-3 (special reserve bank account for the exclusive benefit of customers) to accounts maintained in the bank's trust department. OCC Interpretive Letter No. 1078 (April 19, 2007).

– *Fees for Admissions and Withdrawals from Model-Driven Funds.* A national bank may continue to charge fees for admissions and withdrawals from its model-driven funds for a 90-day period following its affiliate's proposed acquisition of the benchmark indices used for the funds, provided that the bank continues to operate separately from the affiliate. The OCC agreed to review the matter after the acquisition to determine whether the bank could continue its activities after the 90-day period. OCC Interpretive Letter No. 1119 (September 19, 2008).

– *Investment of Employees Benefit Account Assets.* A national bank may invest assets of tax-exempt employee benefit accounts held by the bank in any capacity (including agent), in part 9 collective investment funds, provided the fund itself is exempt from federal taxation. OCC Interpretive Letter No. 884 (January 13, 2000).

– *Nationwide Trust Services.* A national banks with fiduciary powers may serve trust customers nationwide, including at trust representatives offices where the bank performs services for trust customers, but does not conduct any core activities that would deem it to be a branch—receive deposits, pay checks, or lend money—without regard to state requirements that restrict entry, offices, marketing, or otherwise attempt to limit the exercise of lawful national bank fiduciary business, including licensing requirements. OCC Interpretive Letter No. 866, reprinted in [Current

Transfer Binder] Fed. Banking L. Rep. (CCH) ¶ 81,360; (October 8, 1999); OCC Interpretive Letter No. 872, reprinted in [Current Transfer Binder] Fed. Banking L. Rep. (CCH) ¶ 81,366 (October 28, 1999).

– *Real Estate Brokerage and Related Activities as a Fiduciary.* A national bank with fiduciary powers may engage in certain real estate brokerage and related activities as a fiduciary (e.g., management of real property as agent or trustee for its customers). OCC Interpretive Letter (December 20, 1990), OCC Interpretive Letter (September 13, 1984), OCC Interpretive Letter (July 14, 1983).

– *Redemption Requests From Collective Investment Fund.* A national bank may extend the time period allowable for satisfying redemption requests from participants in the bank's collective investment fund. The fund held primarily commercial real estate assets and, because of current economic and market conditions and the large volume of redemption requests the bank was unable to satisfy all the requests within the one year notice period required by the OCC. OCC Interpretive Letter No. 1121 (June 18, 2009).

– *Self-Deposit in Short-Term Investment Fund.* A national bank may pool individual fiduciary accounts awaiting investment or distribution and self- deposit them in a short-term investment fund. Assuming applicable law in states in which the bank does business and plans to self-deposit does not prohibit such deposits, 12 CFR 9.10(b) provides the applicable authority required by 12 CFR 9.12 for the bank to self-deposit such funds or to deposit them with affiliates. OCC Interpretive Letter No. 969 (April 28, 2003).

Insurance and Annuities Activities

- **Bank-Owned Life Insurance (BOLI)**. A national bank may continue to hold a separate account BOLI investment that in turns holds interests in instruments with characteristics of debt securities and a rate of return, a portion of which is linked to equity securities, provided the bank's examiner in charge has no supervisory objection. OCC Interpretive Letter No. 1030 (May 26, 2005).

- **Excess Lines Insurance**. Following the merger of a state-chartered bank into a national bank, the national bank may retain an operating subsidiary of the former state bank that provides "excess lines" insurance coverage for the parent bank. That is, the subsidiary provides liability insurance for the parent bank in excess of the limits for the bank's primary liability insurance that is obtained from a third party. This is an "authorized product" within the meaning of section 302 of the Gramm-Leach-Bliley Act of 1999. CRA Decision 125 (December 21, 2004).

- **Homeowners Insurance Products**. A situation involving a particular solicitation letter offering homeowners insurance products to loan customers of a national bank subsidiary does not involve a prohibited tying arrangement under 12 USC 1972. OCC Interpretive Letter No. 991 (March 11, 2004).

- **Insurance Consumer Protections**. Responses to questions relating to retail sales practices, solicitations, advertising or offers of insurance products and annuities by depository institutions. "Interagency Guidance on Consumer Protections for Depository Institution Sales of Insurance," OCC Bulletin 2001-43 (August 17, 2001).

- **Insurance Information-Sharing Agreements**. The OCC entered into insurance information-sharing agreements with insurance regulators of nine additional states in 2003. As of the end of 2003, only two states (Massachusetts and Rhode Island) and Puerto Rico do not have such agreements with the OCC.

- **Workers' Compensation Self-Insurance**. A national bank may participate in a group to self-insure group members' workers' compensation obligations. OCC Interpretive Letter No. 1022 (February 15, 2005).

Insurance Underwriting and Reinsurance

- **Captive Insurance Company/Underwriting Insurance Coverage on the Operating Risks of the Parent Bank and Its Affiliates**. A national bank may establish an operating subsidiary to serve as a captive insurance company to underwrite insurance coverages on the operating risks of the parent bank and its affiliates. Corporate Decision 99-03, 1999 OCC QJ LEXIS 97 (June 1999); OCC Interpretive Letter No. 845, reprinted in [1998-1999 Transfer Binder] Fed. Banking L. Rep. (CCH) ¶ 81, 300 (October 20, 1998).

- **Credit Life Insurance**. In addition to acting as agent, national banks may provide credit life and disability insurance to loan customers. National banks may also underwrite credit life, accident, health, disability and involuntary unemployment insurance; mortgage life and disability insurance; and mortgage bond insurance. National banks may reinsure credit life, accident, health, disability and involuntary unemployment insurance; mortgage life, mortgage accidental death, and mortgage disability insurance; and mortgage insurance. 12 USC 24(Seventh); Conditional Approval No. 334, 1999 OCC QJ LEXIS 75 (October 30, 1999); Corporate Decisions 98-31 (May 26, 1998), 98-28 (May 11, 1998), 97-92 (October 17, 1997), 1998 OCC QJ LEXIS 189 (September 1998); Conditional Approval No. 259 (October 31, 1997).

- **Disclosure for Renewals of Insurance Policies**. Section 305 of the Gramm-Leach-Bliley Act and implementing regulations do not mandate that banks provide disclosures for renewals of insurance policies sold prior to October 1, 2001. OCC Interpretive Letter No. 960 (February 28, 2003).

- **Grandfathered Insurance Products Sales**. National banks and their subsidiaries may continue to underwrite any "insurance" products being provided by national banks as of 1/1/99 or that were authorized in writing by the Comptroller as of that date. 15 USC 6712 (as added by section 302 of the Gramm-Leach-Bliley Act).

- **National Trust Companies/Sale of Insurance**. National trust companies may sell insurance from a trust office located in a place of 5,000 if the office performs core fiduciary functions, including accepting fiduciary appointments, executing trust documents, and making decisions regarding the investment and distribution of fiduciary assets. OCC Interpretive Letter No. 877, reprinted in [Current Transfer Binder] Fed. Banking L. Rep. (CCH) ¶ 81,371 (December 13, 1999).

- **Place of 5000**. A national bank may sell insurance directly or through and "operating subsidiary" if the national bank is located and doing business in a place of 5,000 or less in population and its agency is also located in that place. 12 USC 92.

- **"Place" for Purposes of "5000 or Less in Population."** Any area designated by the Census Bureau as a "place" is a "place" for purposes of section 92. OCC Interpretive Letter No. 823,reprinted in [1997-98 Transfer Binder] Fed. Banking L. Rep. (CCH) ¶ 81,272 (February 27, 1998).

- **Risk Management Activities**. Risk management activities are part of an insurance agency's activities. A national bank is not required to file a new financial subsidiary notice with the OCC if the bank's existing insurance agency financial subsidiaries provide risk management services as part of their insurance agency activities. OCC Interpretive Letter No. 967 (June 6, 2003).

- **Safe Deposit Box Liability Insurance**. A national bank may underwrite safe deposit box liability insurance for the safe deposit boxes of the bank and its affiliates. Corporate Decision No. 97-92 (October 17, 1997), 1998 OCC QJ LEXIS 189.

- **Sale of Annuities**. National banks may sell annuities without regard to the place- of-5,000 restriction in 12 USC 92 on sale of insurance products. NationsBank v. Variable Annuity Life Insurance Co., 513 US 251 (1995).

- **Satellite Offices**. National banks and their subsidiaries with insurance agencies may rely on OCC opinions to establish satellite offices outside the place of 5,000 (including satellite offices in states outside the state where the insurance business is located) to solicit and sell insurance in the same manner generally permissible for state insurance agencies. OCC Interpretive Letter No. 882 (February 22, 2000); OCC Interpretive Letter No. 864, reprinted in [Current Transfer Binder] Fed. Banking L. Rep. (CCH) ¶ 81,358 (May 19, 1999); OCC Interpretive Letter No. 873, reprinted in [Current Transfer Binder] Fed. Banking L. Rep. (CCH) ¶ 81,360 (December 1, 1999); OCC Interpretive Letter No. 844, reprinted in [Current Transfer Binder] Fed. Banking L. Rep. (CCH) ¶ 81,367 (October 20, 1998)

- **Scope of Market**. A national bank generally may sell insurance pursuant to section 92 in the same nationwide market as is generally available to licensed insurance agencies in the state where the bank agency operates. OCC Interpretive Letter No. 753, reprinted in [1996-1997 Transfer Binder] Fed. Banking L. Rep. (CCH) 81,107 (November 4, 1996).

- **Scope of Sales/Domicile of Customers**. A national bank may sell insurance to customers wherever the customers are located. See NBD Bank, N.A. v. Bennett, 67 F.3d 629 (7th

Cir. 1995); Independent Insurance Agent of America, Inc. v. Ludwig, 997 F.2d 958 (D.C. Cir. 1993); Shawmut Bank Connecticut v. Googins, 965 F. Supp. 304 (D. Conn. 1997).

- **Title Insurance; Sales Pursuant to 15 USC 6713 (GLBA section 303)**. National banks may sell title insurance as agent in the same manner and to the same extent in a given state as state banks are authorized to sell title insurance in that state. A grandfather provision permits a national bank and its subsidiary to continue to conduct title insurance activities that they were actively and lawfully conducting before November 12, 1999. 15 USC 6713.

- **Underwriting Credit-Related Insurance Post–GLBA**. A national bank's operating subsidiary may continue underwriting credit-related insurance products in connection with loans made by the bank and affiliated and unaffiliated financial institution lenders under the "authorized product" exception of section 302 of the Gramm-Leach-Bliley Act (GLBA). OCC Interpretive Letter No. 886 (March 27, 2000).

- **Reinsurance**

  - *Mortgage Insurance*. National banks may collectively own, with other financial institutions, a mortgage reinsurance company that provides mortgage reinsurance on the loans of the participating financial institutions and their affiliates and subsidiaries. The national bank participants may make a noncontrolling investment in the mortgage reinsurance company using the notice procedure available under the OCC's regulations at 12 CFR 5.36(e), if the bank otherwise qualifies under the criteria of that section. OCC Interpretive Letter No. 985 (January 14, 2004).

  - *Mortgage Reinsurance*. A national bank may reinsure mortgage insurance on loans originated, purchased, or serviced by the bank, its subsidiaries, or its affiliates. 12 CFR 5.34, Corporate Decision No. 99-02 (December 11, 1998). A national bank's captive mortgage reinsurance subsidiary may enter a mortgage reinsurance agreement with a Cayman Islands segregated portfolio company to reinsure private mortgage insurance on loans originated or purchased by the bank or one of its affiliates. OCC Interpretive Letter No. 862, reprinted in [Current Transfer Binder] Fed. Banking L. Rep. (CCH) ¶ 81,356 (June 7, 1999).

  - *Mortgage Reinsurance Exchange*. National banks may participate in a mortgage reinsurance exchange where the exchange will provide for the reinsurance of private mortgage insurance on loans originated or purchased by participating lenders. OCC Interpretive Letter No. 828, reprinted in [1997-1998 Transfer Binder] Fed. Banking L. Rep. (CCH) ¶ 81,277 (April 6, 1998).

  - *Municipal Bond Insurance*. National banks may underwrite municipal bond insurance. OCC Interpretive Letter No. 338, reprinted in [1985-1987 Transfer Binder] Fed. Banking L. Rep. (CCH) ¶ 85,508 (May 2, 1985); American Insurance Association v. Clarke, 656 F. Supp. 404 (D.D.C. 1987), aff'd, 865 F.2d 278 (D.C. Cir. 1989).

- *Reinsurance Activities of Credit-Related Insurance for Unaffiliated Lenders.* A national bank operating subsidiary may provide reinsurance of credit life, health and disability insurance written in connection with loans extended by a bank and affiliated and unaffiliated lenders under the "authorized product" exception of section 302 of the Gramm-Leach-Bliley Act. Corporate Decision No. 2001-10 (April 23, 2001).

- *Reinsurance (and Underwriting) of Credit Life Insurance, Credit Disability, and/or Involuntary Unemployment Insurance.* National banks may reinsure (and underwrite) credit life insurance, credit disability, credit accident, credit health, and/or involuntary unemployment insurance sold to customers that borrow from the bank and/or its lending affiliates and/or subsidiaries. Corporate Decision Nos. Corporate Decision No. 98-31, (May 26, 1998), 98-28 (May 11, 1998).

- *Reinsurance of Credit Life and Other Insurance Post–GLBA.* A national bank may establish an operating subsidiary to reinsure credit life, accident, disability, and health insurance in connection with loans made by the bank and its affiliates, because the reinsurance of credit-related insurance products satisfies the "authorized product" exception of section 302 of the Gramm-Leach-Bliley Act. Corporate Decision No. 2000-16 (August 29, 2000).

- *Reinsuring Mortgage Insurance.* National banks may collectively own, with other financial institutions, a mortgage reinsurance company that provides mortgage reinsurance on the loans of the participating financial institutions and their affiliates and subsidiaries. The national bank participants may make a noncontrolling investment in the mortgage reinsurance company using the notice procedure available under the OCC's regulations at 12 CFR 5.36(e), if the bank otherwise qualifies under the criteria of that section. OCC Interpretive Letter No. 985 (January 14, 2004).

Title Insurance

- **Title Insurance, in General.** Unless a state law in effect before November 12, 1999 prohibits all persons in a state from selling or underwriting title insurance:

  - *Grandfathered Title Insurance Activities.* A national bank and its subsidiaries may continue to conduct title insurance activities, including underwriting, in which the national bank or subsidiary were lawfully engaged before November 12, 1999, subject to some exceptions if affiliates are providing insurance as principal. 15 USC 6713 (as added by section 303 of GLBA).

  - *Sales as Agent.* National banks and their subsidiaries may sell title insurance as agents in a state to the same extent as permitted for state banks. 15 USC 6713 (as added by section 303 of GLBA).

  - *State Parity for Title Insurance Sales Through an Operating Subsidiary.* National bank's operating subsidiary could sell title insurance in Pennsylvania, without being subject to the place of 5000 requirement, because state law permits title insurance sales without geographic limitations. Conditional Approval No. 371 (March 20, 2000).

- **Title Insurance Sales Through a Financial Subsidiary**. Financial subsidiary of a national bank may offer title insurance in the State of New Jersey, even though New Jersey law generally prohibits banks from selling title insurance. Corporate Decision No. 2000-14 (August 16, 2000).

Securities Activities

- **Asset Securitization**. National banks may purchase and sell, as principal or agent, asset-backed obligations. 12 CFR 1.2(l), (m). National banks may securitize and sell assets they hold, including mortgage and nonmortgage loans that are originated by the bank or purchased from others. National banks may buy and sell as principal asset-backed obligations. 12 CFR 1.3(g).

- **Auction Rate Preferred Securities**. A wholly owned subsidiary of a national bank may purchase and hold for its own account shares of certain preferred auction rate securities as investment securities for the purposes of 12 CFR 1, subject to certain enforceable conditions under 12 USC 1818. The subsidiary agreed to not exercise certain voting rights under the securities. The subsidiary and the bank were required to enter into an operating agreement with the OCC and an indemnification agreement with the bank's holding company. The subsidiary agreed to hold the securities for a limited period of time, after which the holding company will be required to repurchase the securities. The holding company agreed to indemnify the bank against certain potential losses in connection with these purchases. The bank must seek prior OCC supervisory no-objection before terminating, modifying, or amending the agreements described in the letter. OCC Interpretive Letter No. 1115 (April 3, 2009); see also OCC Interpretive Letter No. 1124 (November 3, 2009).

- **Broker-Dealer Activities**. National banks directly, and without registering with the SEC, may engage in many types of securities broker-dealer activities, including transactions for trust customers, private placements, issuance and sales of certain asset-backed securities, transactions for certain stock purchase plans, and transactions in "identified banking products" (including generally deposit instruments, banker's acceptances, loan participations (subject to certain sales restrictions), and derivatives). 15 USC 78c(a)(4), (5) (as amended by sections 201 and 202 of GLBA).

- **Clearing and Execution Services**. National banks may execute and clear securities transactions. OCC Interpretive Letter No. 494, reprinted in [1989-1990 Transfer Binder] Fed. Banking L. Rep. (CCH) ¶ 83,038 (December 20, 1989).

- **Closed End Mutual Funds**. National banks may organize a closed end investment company (which does not continuously offer shares for purchase). OCC Conditional Approval No. 164 (December 9, 1994).

- **Deposit Notes Do Not Constitute "Securities."** Sales of a national bank's deposit notes through its affiliated retail securities broker-dealer network do not constitute the sale of "securities" as defined in OCC securities offering regulations at 12 CFR 16. OCC Interpretive Letter No. 922 (December 13, 2001).

- **Derivatives Activities**. National banks may offer investment advice and engage in a variety of derivative activities (including swaps, futures, forwards, and options) as a financial intermediary or to manage or reduce risks.

- **FDIC Temporary Liquidity Guarantee Program**. The guarantee of a qualifying debt security by the FDIC under its Temporary Liquidity Guarantee Program transforms a qualifying security into a Type 1 security for purposes of 12 CFR 1. In cases where the security's tenor is coextensive with the term of the guarantee, the security qualifies as a Type 1 security. In cases where the security's tenor exceeds the term of the FDIC guarantee, the security does not qualify as a Type 1 security. OCC Interpretive Letter No. 1109 (January 8, 2009).

- **Financial Warranties in Connection With a Mutual Fund**. A national bank and its wholly owned subsidiary may provide financial warranties under 12 CFR 1017 in connection with a specified mutual fund, under the specific facts described and subject to satisfying the safety and soundness considerations discussed. The circumstances involve a factually complex financial transaction. The financial warranties, in effect, guarantee that the investment structuring advice and asset allocation monitoring services provided by the bank in the creation and operation of the fund will result in the designed return to investors. Known in the industry as "principal protected" funds, the fund is designed so that investors will not lose any principal over a designated holding period and will earn a minimum fixed rate of return. OCC Interpretive Letter No. 1010 (September 7, 2004).

- **Investment Advisory Activities With Limited Interest in Advised Funds**. A national bank may acquire a noncontrolling investment in an SEC-registered investment advisory company, when the investment advisory company owns limited equity interests in investment funds to which it provides investment advisory and related services, if the limited interests are necessary for the company to engage in bank permissible investment advisory activities due to investor demands, industry practices, and competitive factors. OCC Interpretive Letter No. 897 (October 23, 2000).

- **Investment Vehicle for Bank Clients**. A national bank's operating subsidiary, a limited liability company (LLC), may serve as a sole general partner of a limited partnership that is used as an investment vehicle for bank clients. Corporate Decision No. 2000-07 (May 10, 2000).

- **Limited Equity Investment in Connection With Investment Management Activities**. The OCC approved a national bank application to establish a third-tier financial subsidiary to serve as the general partner of a newly formed private investment fund and to allow the financial subsidiary, or its direct parent subsidiary, to hold a limited equity interest in the fund in connection with the subsidiary's investment management activities.

Holding this interest is an integral part of the compensation structure for investment advisers to private investment funds, and this investment is permissible as an activity that is incidental to the authority of a national bank's subsidiary to provide investment advisory services. OCC Conditional Approval No. 819 (September 7, 2007).

- **Lobby Leasing and Employee Sharing Arrangements**. National banks may engage in various lobby leasing and employee sharing arrangements that provide full service brokerage and investment advice to customers through use of third-party providers. 12 CFR 7.3001; OCC Interpretive Letter No. (June 4, 1985); OCC Interpretive Letter No. 407, reprinted in [1988-1989 Transfer Binder] Fed. Banking L. Rep. (CCH) ¶ 85,631 (August 4, 1987). 15 USC 78(c)(a)(4)(B)(i) (as amended by section 201 of the Gramm-Leach-Bliley Act).

- **Loss Allocation Systems**. A national bank may become a member of the Government Securities Division of the Fixed Income Clearing Corporation and participate in its loss allocation system. OCC Interpretive Letter No. 1014 (January 10, 2005).

- **Municipal Securities**. National banks may underwrite, deal in, and act as agent in the purchase and sale of general obligation bonds. They may also underwrite, deal in, and act as agent in the purchase and sale of revenue bonds if they are well capitalized. 12 USC 24(Seventh).

- **Mutual Fund Activities**. National banks and their operating subsidiaries may offer a broad range of administrative and investment advisory services, serve as custodian and transfer agent, and broker investment company shares. OCC Interpretive Letter No. 648, reprinted in [1994 Transfer Binder] Fed. Banking L. Rep. (CCH) ¶ 83,557 (May 4, 1994).

- **Networking Arrangements**. National banks may enter into networking arrangements, whereby securities brokerage services are made available to bank customers by a broker dealer using leased space on bank premises. OCC Interpretive Letters Nos. 406-408, reprinted in [1988-1989 Transfer Binder] Fed. Banking L. Rep. (CCH) 55,630 to 85,632 (August 4, 1987).

- **Online Securities Trading**. A national bank may acquire an indirect noncontrolling interest in an entity that will provide online securities trading and related services. In general, the bank should indicate that it does not provide, endorse, or guarantee any of the products or services available through the third-party Web pages. For links to pages that provide non-deposit investment products, the disclosures also should alert customers to risks associated with these products, for example, by stating that the products are not insured by the FDIC, are not a deposit, and may lose value. Banks also have responsibility for the appropriate placement of disclosures via electronic means on their Web page(s). OCC Interpretive Letter No. 889 (April 24, 2000).

- **Options on Futures Contracts**. A national bank may purchase options on futures contracts on commodities to hedge the credit risk in its agricultural loan portfolio. OCC Interpretive Letter No. 896 (August 21, 2000).

- **Parent Bank's Investment Securities Portfolio**. A national bank operating subsidiary may own, hold, and manage all or part of the parent bank's investment securities portfolio. 12 CFR 5.34(ii)(N).

- **Performance-Linked Compensation**. National banks may offer products and services and may accept as sole or partial compensation a share of the customer's profit, income, or earnings. Such performance-linked compensation can be in the form of stock warrants or contractual arrangements between the bank and its customer, whereby a share of the customer's profits, income, or earnings would be paid to the bank. 12 CFR 7.1006; Corporate Decision No. 2000-02 (February 25, 2000).

- **Private Placement of Securities**. National banks may privately place securities. Securities Industry Association v. Board of Governors, Federal Reserve, 807 F.2d 1052 (D.C. Cir. 1986), cert. denied, 483 U.S. 1005 (1987) ("Bankers Trust II").

- **Private Placement Services**. A national bank's operating subsidiary may assist customers in the issuance of debt and equity securities by providing private placement services as agent, and financial and transactional advice to customers in structuring, arranging and executing various financial transactions, as agent, in connection with its private placement activities. While performance-linked compensation, including warrants, may be accepted as the compensation for such services, neither the bank nor the subsidiary may exercise any warrants. Corporate Decision No. 2000-02 (February 25, 2000).

- **Repurchase Obligations**. National banks may purchase securities subject to repurchase agreements. OCC Interpretive Letter No. 629, reprinted in [1993-1994 Transfer Binder] Fed. Banking L. Rep. (CCH) ¶ 83,512 (July 2, 1993).

- **Resecuritization of Residential Mortgage-Backed Securities**. National banks may resecuritize certain residential mortgage-backed securities under 12 CFR 1 and 12 USC 24(Seventh), but are subject to various terms and conditions and the accuracy of representations. OCC Interpretive Letter 1133 (June 16, 2011).

- **Riskless Principal**. National banks may act as riskless principal in securities transactions. OCC Interpretive Letter No. 626, reprinted in [1993-1994 Transfer Binder] Fed. Banking L. Rep. (CCH) 83, 508 (July 7, 1993).

- **Securities Brokerage**. National banks may provide full service securities brokerage (investment advisory services and brokerage services) or act as a futures commission merchant, and provide credit and other related services. 12 USC 24(Seventh).

- **Securities Brokerage in Primary Markets**. A national bank's broker-dealer subsidiary may act as a broker for securities underwritten by a section 20 affiliate. A federal branch may act as a broker for 144A securities initially purchased by its foreign parent. OCC Interpretive Letter No. 876 (December 8, 1999), reprinted in [1999-2000 Transfer Binder] Fed. Banking L. Rep. (CCH) ¶ 881-370; Letter from Julie L. Williams, Chief

Counsel, dated January 26, 1999; Letter from Julie L. Williams, Chief Counsel, dated February 25, 1998.

- **Securities Conduit Lending Services**. A national bank may engage in securities lending activities as custodian to various institutional customers as well as to customers for whom the bank may not be custodian (on a third-party agency basis). The bank may offer its custodial and non-custodial customers various programs to assist the customer in enhancing the return on the securities, including conduit lending, whereby the bank's customer chooses various potential borrowers of custodial funds from a list of potential borrowers. The bank is appointed as an agent of the customer in order to find borrowers for the customer's lendable securities. OCC Interpretive Letter No. 1026 (April 27, 2005).

- **Securities Confirmation Rules**. A national bank may request a waiver from the OCC of certain provisions of the OCC's securities confirmation rules in connection with the bank's transfer agent activities for various dividend reinvestment, stock purchase, and employee stock purchase plans. OCC Interpretive Letter No. 1029 (May 23, 2005).

- **Securities Exchanges**. A national bank's operating subsidiary may join domestic exchanges and clearinghouses, provided that the bank and its subsidiaries do not guarantee or otherwise become liable for trades executed and/or cleared, the national bank does not guarantee or assume liability for the operating subsidiary, and the national bank complies with certain conditions. OCC Interpretive Letter Nos. 624, reprinted in [1993-1994 Transfer Binder] Fed. Banking L. Rep. (CCH) ¶ 83,506 (June 30, 1993); 629, reprinted in [1993-1994 Transfer Binder] Fed. Banking L. Rep. (CCH) ¶ 83,512 (July 2, 1993); 494, reprinted in [1989-1990 Transfer Binder] Fed. Banking L. Rep. (CCH) ¶ 5 8,707 (December 20, 1990); 293, reprinted in [1993-1994 Transfer Binder] Fed. Banking L. Rep. (CCH) ¶58,707 (May 21, 1986).

- **Securities Lending**. National banks may lend securities from their own investment or trading accounts or from safekeeping, trust, or pension accounts of their customers. Banking Circular No. 196 (May 7, 1985).

- **Securities Transactions Reports**. For a national bank that has both manual and automated processes to track employee securities trades, Part 12 requirements that certain covered bank officers and employees report to the bank within 10 business days after the end of the calendar quarter all personal transactions in securities made by them in which they have a beneficial interest are waived. The bank receives all necessary data more promptly than the rule requires, either directly from its brokerage affiliate or through duplicate brokerage statements and confirmations of individual trades that the bank receives from other brokerages. OCC Interpretive Letter No. 1011 (October 4, 2004).

- **Sweeps**. National banks may sweep funds from a corporate demand deposit account to a proprietary money market account. OCC Interpretive Letter No. 760, reprinted in [1996-1997 Transfer Binder] Fed. Banking L. Rep. (CCH) ¶ 81,124 (November 14, 1996), 688, reprinted in [1995-1996 Transfer Binder] Fed. Banking L. Rep. (CCH) ¶ 81,003 (May 31, 1995).

- **Transfer Agent**. National banks may act as a transfer or fiscal agent and may guarantee the signature of an endorser or transferor of securities. 15 USC 78q-1, 12 CFR 9.20; OCC Interpretive Letter. (December 5, 1985).

- **Trust Bank Subsidiary and Limited Equity Investment Incident to Investment Management Activities**. The OCC conditionally approved a national bank's application to establish a limited-purpose national trust bank as a subsidiary and for the trust bank to establish an operating subsidiary that would organize and manage two private investment funds. In connection with the operating subsidiary's investment management activities, it would hold special limited- equity interests in the two private investment funds. Holding such interests is an integral part of the compensation structure for investment advisers to private investment funds, and this investment is permissible as an activity that is incidental to the authority of a national bank's subsidiary to provide investment advisory services. The conditional approval also required the trust bank to maintain minimum capital and liquidity levels, to implement systems and controls to manage risks associated with organizing and managing private investment funds, to notify the OCC of the departure of the investment manager of the operating subsidiary, and to notify OCC of changes in the trust bank's business plan. OCC Conditional Approval No. 804 (May 1, 2007).

- **Underwriting and Dealing**. National banks directly, and through operating subsidiaries, may underwrite, deal in, and act as agent in the purchase and sale of various types of securities, including U.S. government securities, municipal general obligation and revenue bonds, and asset-backed securities. 12 USC 24(Seventh); 12 CFR 12; 12 CFR 1.

Derivatives

- **Derivatives, in General**. National banks and their operating subsidiaries may advise, structure, arrange, and execute transactions, as agent or principal, in connection with interest rate, basis rate, currency, currency coupon, and cash- settled commodity, commodity price index, equity and equity index swaps, and other related derivative products, such as caps, collars, floors, swaptions, forward rate agreements, and other similar products commonly known as derivatives. National banks may originate, trade, and make markets in these products. National banks may arrange matched swaps or enter into unmatched swaps on an individual or portfolio basis and may offset unmatched positions with exchange- traded futures and options contracts or over-the-counter cash-settled options. National banks may provide financial advice and counseling for these activities as permissible incidental activities under 12 USC 24(Seventh). OCC Interpretive Letter No. 725, reprinted in [1995-1996 Transfer Binder] Fed. Banking L. Rep. (CCH) ¶ 81,040 (May 10, 1996).

  - *Cash-Settled Options and Forwards on Equity Securities*. A national bank may engage in cash-settled options and forwards on equity securities if part of the bank's customer-driven, non-proprietary financial intermediation business and if the bank has in place an appropriate risk management and measurement process for its derivative and hedging activities. OCC Interpretive Letter No. 949 (September 19, 2002).

– *Customer-Driven Derivatives Transactions—Inflation Indices.* A national bank may engage in customer-driven, perfectly matched, cash-settled derivative transactions on inflation indices. Before the bank may engage in the transactions, the bank must notify its Examiner-in-Charge (EIC), in writing, of the proposed activities and must receive written notification of the EIC's supervisory no-objection, based on the EIC's evaluation of the adequacy of the bank's risk measurement and management systems and controls to enable the bank to engage in the proposed activities on a safe and sound basis, and the EIC's evaluation of any other supervisory considerations relevant to the particular proposal. OCC Interpretive Letter No. 1079 (April 19, 2007).

– *Customer-Driven Derivatives Transactions—Metal Derivatives.* National banks and certain foreign (London) branches may engage in customer- driven, metal derivative transactions that settle in cash or by transitory title transfer and that are hedged on a portfolio basis with derivatives that settle in cash or by transitory title transfer. OCC Interpretive Letter No. 1073 (October 19, 2006).

– *Customer-Driven Derivatives Transactions—Specified Property Indices.* A national bank may engage in customer-driven, perfectly matched, cash- settled derivative transactions on certain specified property indices. Before the bank may engage in the transactions, the bank must notify its Examiner-in-Charge (EIC), in writing, of the proposed activities and must receive written notification of the EIC's supervisory no-objection, based on the EIC's evaluation of the adequacy of the bank's risk measurement and management systems and controls to enable the bank to engage in the proposed activities on a safe and sound basis, and the EIC's evaluation of any other supervisory considerations relevant to the particular proposal. OCC Interpretive Letter No. 1081 (May 15, 2007).

– *Customer-Driven Property Index Derivatives Transactions—Broad-Based Property Indices.* A national bank may engage in customer-driven, perfectly matched, cash-settled property index derivative transactions on regularly produced broad-based property indices that use appraisal- and sales-based data on foreign and domestic commercial and residential real estate. Before the bank may engage in these transactions, the bank must notify its Examiner-in-Charge (EIC), in writing, of the proposed activities and must receive written notification of the EIC's supervisory no-objection. OCC Interpretive Letter No. 1089 (October 15, 2007.)

– *Debt Cancellation Contracts Offered Through Automobile Dealers.* A national bank is authorized to offer debt cancellation contracts (DCC) to consumers through automobile dealers by 12 USC 24(Seventh) and 12 CFR 37, and the DCCs are subject to the standards of part 37 as well. However, when a national bank's DCC provides protection on a closed- end loan repayable in five years, the bank cannot collect the full cost of the DCC in monthly periodic payments over the first year of the loan. To comply with the periodic payment option under section 37.5, the bank must collect DCC fees in periodic payments (i) over the full 5-year term of the loan, or (ii) until such time as the loan is repaid. OCC Interpretive Letter No. 1095 (February 27, 2008).

– *Derivatives Transactions.* A national trust company may use cash-settled derivatives linked to the S&P 500 Index to hedge the market risk associated with the fees it charges customers as part of its investment advisory activities, provided the trust company establishes, to the satisfaction of its supervisory office, an appropriate risk management and compliance process. OCC Interpretive Letter No. 1037 (August 9, 2005).

– *Derivatives Transactions.* A national bank may engage in customer- driven, perfectly matched, cash-settled derivatives transactions provided the bank's Examiner-in-Charge is satisfied that the bank has adequate risk management and measurement systems and controls to conduct the activities on a safe and sound basis. OCC Interpretive Letter No. 1039 (September 13, 2005).

– *Derivatives Transactions—Below-Investment Grade Bonds.* A national bank may hedge the risks arising from bank permissible, customer-driven derivative transactions using below-investment grade bonds. However, before the bank commences the proposed activities, the bank's examiner- in-charge must be satisfied that the bank has adequate risk management and measurement systems and controls to conduct the activities on a safe and sound basis. The limitations of 12 CFR Part 1 applicable to investment securities would not apply to these transactions, rather the transactions would be subject to standards applicable to derivatives activities. OCC Interpretive Letter No. 1064 (July 13, 2006).

– *Derivatives Transactions—Frozen Concentrate Orange Juice, Polypropylene.* A national bank may engage in customer-driven, perfectly matched, cash-settled derivative transactions on frozen concentrate orange juice, low density polyethylene and polypropylene, and certain reference assets permitted under OCC Interpretive Letter No. 1039 (September 13, 2005), provided the bank's Examiner-in-Charge is satisfied that the bank has adequate risk management and measurement systems and controls to conduct the activities on a safe and sound basis. OCC Interpretive Letter No. 1056 (March 29, 2006).

– *Derivatives Transactions—Hogs, Lumber, Corrugated Cardboard, Polystyrene.* A national bank may engage in customer-driven, perfectly matched, cash-settled derivative transactions (such as swaps, options, forwards, caps, floors, collars and futures) where payments are based on prices of (i) hogs (including pork bellies), (ii) lumber, (iii) corrugated cardboard (including new and recycled), and (iv) polystyrene. Before doing so, however, the bank's Examiner-in-Charge must be satisfied that the bank has adequate risk management and measurement systems and controls to conduct the activities on a safe and sound basis. OCC Interpretive Letter No. 1063 (June 1, 2006).

– *Derivatives Transactions—Metal*. A national bank and its London branch may engage in customer-driven, metal derivative transactions that settle in cash or by transitory title transfer and that are hedged on a portfolio basis with derivatives that settle in cash or by transitory title transfer. Before the bank may engage in these transactions, the bank must notify its examiner- in-charge (EIC), in writing, of the proposed activities and must receive written notification of the EIC's supervisory non-objection. OCC Interpretive Letter No. 1073 (October 19, 2006).

– *Derivatives Transactions—Polypropylene, Corrugated Cardboard, Dow Jones AIG Commodity Index*. A national bank may engage in customer- driven, perfectly matched, cash-settled derivative transactions (such as swaps, options, forwards, caps, floors, collars and futures) where payments are based on prices of (i) polypropylene: injection molding (copoly), (ii) old corrugated cardboard #11, and (iii) the Dow Jones AIG Commodity Index, provided the bank's Examiner-in-Charge is satisfied that the bank has adequate risk management and measurement systems and controls to conduct the activities on a safe and sound basis. OCC Interpretive Letter No. 1059 (April 13, 2006).

– *Derivatives Transactions—Portfolio-Hedged Coal Derivatives*. A national bank may engage in customer-driven coal derivative transactions that settle in cash or by transitory title transfer and that are hedged on a portfolio basis with derivative and spot transactions that settle in cash or by transitory title transfer, provided the bank's Examiner-in-Charge is satisfied that the bank has adequate risk management and measurement systems and controls to conduct the activities on a safe and sound basis. OCC Interpretive Letter No. 1060 (April 26, 2006).

– *Derivatives Transactions—Reference Assets and Related Indices*. A national bank may engage in customer-driven, perfectly matched, cash- settled derivative transactions with payments based on 11 categories of commodities reference assets/ related indices. Before a national bank may engage in such transactions on reference assets not previously reviewed by the bank's Examiner-in-Charge (EIC), the bank must notify its EIC, in writing, of the proposed activities and must receive written notification of the EIC's supervisory non-objection, based on the EIC's evaluation of the adequacy of the bank's risk measurement and management systems and controls to enable the bank to engage in the proposed activities on a safe and sound basis, and the EIC's evaluation of any other supervisory considerations relevant to the particular proposal. OCC Interpretive Letter No. 1065 (July 24, 2006).

– *Derivative Transactions Referencing Longevity Indices*. A national bank may act as a financial intermediary in customer-driven, perfectly matched, cash-settled derivative transactions referencing longevity indices. The derivatives involve making financial payments based on the performance of indices that track mortality and longevity data of national populations. The bank's role is to negotiate a financial contract with one customer and an offsetting contract with a second customer. By engaging in the described activities, the bank will not be providing insurance in a state as principal, as generally prohibited by Gramm-Leach-Bliley Act section 302. Before the bank may engage in the transactions, the bank must notify its Examiner-in-Charge, in writing, of the proposed activities and must receive written notification of the EIC's supervisory no-objection. OCC Interpretive Letter No. 1110 (January 30, 2009).

– *Edge Corporation's Holding of Equity Securities for Hedging.* The OCC's limit on a national bank's holding of equity securities for hedging purposes, to 5 percent of a class of stock of any one issuer, does not include securities held by the bank's Edge corporation subsidiary. OCC Interpretive Letter No. 924 (January 2, 2002).

– *Electricity Derivatives.* A national bank may expand its financial intermediation business to include customer-driven, electricity derivative transactions that involve transitory title transfers as an activity incidental to banking, provided the bank has established, to the satisfaction of the OCC, an appropriate risk measurement and management process. OCC Interpretive Letter No. 962 (April 21, 2003).

– *Electricity Derivative and Hedging Activities.* A national bank may conduct customer-driven, cash-settled derivatives business based on electricity prices, and related hedging activities, as an extension of its existing energy-related commodities derivatives business, if the OCC is satisfied that it has an appropriate risk management process for its electricity derivative and hedging activities. OCC Interpretive Letter No. 937 (June 27, 2002).

– *Emissions Derivative Transactions.* A national bank, with the approval of its examiner-in-charge, may engage in customer-driven, physically settled emissions derivative transactions and may enter into physical transactions in emission allowances to hedge its risk exposure to emissions derivative transactions. OCC Interpretive Letter No. 1040 (September 15, 2005).

– *Equity Derivative Transactions.* National banks may engage in equity derivative transactions. National banks may offer time deposit accounts, certificates of deposit, or contracts that pay interest at a rate based on the gain in designated equity indices, including the S&P 500 Index. National banks may engage in swap activities tied to equities and equity indices. A bank may take positions in equities to hedge bank permissible equity derivatives originated by customers for their independent and valid business purposes, if the bank: 1) provides the OCC information about its derivative business and proposed hedging activities, including their effectiveness and efficiency in reducing risks, 2) establishes that the bank has an appropriate risk management process in place, and 3) obtains supervisory approval from the OCC. Decision of the Office of the Comptroller of the Currency on the Request by Chase Manhattan Bank, N.A. to Offer the Chase Market Index Investment Deposit Account (1988); Investment Company Institute v. Ludwig, 884 F. Supp. 4 (D.D.C. 1995); Letter from Ellen Broadman, Director, Securities and Corporate Practices Division, OCC, to Barbara Monheit, Regional Counsel, FDIC (October 29, 1998); OCC Interpretive

Letter No. 652, reprinted in [1994 Transfer Binder] Fed. Banking L. Rep. (CCH) ¶ 83,600 (September 13, 1994); OCC Interpretive Letter No. 892 September 13, 2000), reprinted in [Current Transfer Binder] Fed. Banking L. Rep. (CCH) ¶ 81-4.11.

– *Equity Derivatives Transactions.* A national bank may purchase and hold the following securities to hedge bank permissible equity derivative transactions: common and preferred stock, convertible and exchangeable securities, master limited partnership interests, limited partnership interests, limited liability corporation interests, depositary receipts (including American and Global), closed- and open-end mutual funds, exchange traded funds, and certain real estate investment trusts. Before the bank may engage in physical hedges involving these equity securities for which it has not received a supervisory no-objection, the bank must notify its Examiner-in-Charge (EIC), in writing, and must receive written notification of the EIC's supervisory no-objection. OCC Interpretive Letter No. 1090 (October 25, 2007).

– *Equity Derivative Transactions with Affiliates and Subsidiaries.* A national bank may enter into equity derivatives transactions with certain of its affiliates and subsidiaries that mirror the affiliates' and subsidiaries' transactions with their customers, and the bank may hedge the risks of those transactions in the same manner as it hedges the risks of its existing derivatives business, provided the OCC has no supervisory objection. OCC Interpretive Letter No. 1018 (February 10, 2005).

– *Equity Index Derivatives.* A national bank, with approval of its examiner- in-charge, may engage in customer-driven equity index derivatives transactions and may use baskets of securities to hedge its risk exposures to the index swaps where the baskets do not exactly match the underlying index, but are designed to replicate the sector and industry weightings and general risks of the index. OCC Interpretive Letter No. 1033 (June 14, 2005).

– *Financial Intermediation Transactions Involving Electricity.* A national bank may engage in electricity derivative transactions and hedges, settled in cash and by transitory title transfer, as part of, or incidental to, its existing financial intermediation business in energy-related commodities derivatives, provided the bank has established an appropriate risk measurement and management process for those activities to which the OCC expresses no supervisory objection. OCC Interpretive Letter No. 1025 (April 6, 2005).

– *Financial Intermediation Transactions-Risk Indices Associated with National Events and Catastrophes.* A national bank may act as a financial intermediary in customer-driven, perfectly matched, cash-settled derivative transactions referencing risk indices associated with designated types of natural events and catastrophes. The bank's role is to negotiate a financial contract with one customer and an offsetting contract with a second customer. By engaging in the described activities, the bank will not be providing insurance in a state as principal, as generally prohibited by GLBA section 302. Before the bank may engage in the transactions, the bank must notify its examiner in charge (EIC), in writing, of the proposed activities and must receive written notification of the EIC's supervisory no-objection. OCC Interpretive Letter No. 1101 (July 7, 2008).

– *Foreign Branch Membership in the London Clearing House.* A national bank, via its London branch, may join the London Clearing House as a SwapClear Member to clear interest derivative contracts. OCC Interpretive Letter No. 929 (February 11, 2002).

– *Hedging Credit Risk.* National banks may enter into credit derivative transactions. A national bank may use debt securities that are not investment grade debt securities or the credit equivalents thereof, to hedge bank permissible derivative, including credit derivative, transactions. Banking Bulletin 96-43 (August 12, 1996); Memorandum from Donald N. Lamson, Assistant Director, and Tena M. Alexander, Senior Attorney, Securities and Corporate Practices Division, dated July 26, 2000. A national bank may purchase cash-settled options on futures contracts on bank impermissible commodities to hedge the credit risk in its agricultural loan portfolio. Before a national bank may engage in the activity, the OCC must affirm that the bank has an effective risk management process in place. An effective risk management process includes board supervision, managerial and staff expertise, comprehensive policies and operating procedures, risk identification, measurement and management information systems, as well as effective risk control functions that oversee and ensure the continuing appropriateness of the risk management process. Letter from Julie L. Williams, First Senior Deputy Comptroller and Chief Counsel, dated August 21, 2000.

– *Hedging Risks From Bank Permissible, Customer-Driven Derivative Transactions.* A national bank with an OCC-approved hedging program may execute cash- and physically-settled equity derivative transactions, and use below investment grade bonds to hedge risks arising from permissible derivative transactions done in accordance with the program. A national bank may hedge risks arising from a hedge that remain when a counterparty terminates the underlying hedged transaction. In limited circumstances a national bank may cross-hedge its equity derivatives (i.e., use one security or a basket of securities to hedge the risk arising from a transaction with another, different security, with similar characteristics). OCC Interpretive Letter No. 935 (May 14, 2002).

– *Holding Securities to Hedge Equity Derivatives Transactions.* Subject to supervisory clearance, national banks may take positions in equity securities solely to hedge bank permissible equity derivative transactions originated by customers for their independent business purposes, subject to certain qualifications and quantitative limits. The bank may not hold the securities for speculative purposes. OCC Interpretive Letter No. 892 (September 8, 2000).

– *Hedging With Credit Default Swaps and Below-Investment-Grade Debt.* A national bank may purchase and hold below-investment-grade debt in connection with a comprehensive program to hedge the counterparty credit risk exposure that arises from its derivatives activities. The letter concludes that the bank may engage in the transactions it proposes, where the bank's Examiner-in-Charge is satisfied that the bank has adequate risk management and measurement systems and controls and does not object to the activity. OCC Interpretive Letter No. 1051 (February 15, 2006).

–   *Membership in Independent System Operators and Regional Transmission Operators Organizations.* A national bank may participate as a member in regional Independent System Operators (ISO) and Regional Transmission Operators (RTO) organizations in order to execute electricity derivatives transactions that the OCC previously has found to be permissible for the bank, subject to the limitations set forth in 12 USC 84 and 12 CFR Part 32 and any additional limitations. The bank also is required to notify its EIC and receive written notification of the EIC's supervisory non-objection before becoming a member of an ISO or RTO organization. OCC Interpretive Letter No. 1071 (September 6, 2006).

–   *Membership in IntercontinentalExchange Clear Europe (ICE Europe) Credit Default Swap Clearinghouse.* It is permissible for a national bank to become a credit default swap self-clearing member of ICE Europe, provided the bank has established a comprehensive risk management framework to govern the risks associated with membership, and obtains a written Examiner-in-Charge supervisory no-objection. The bank's exposure to ICE Europe is subject to the lending limit in 12 USC 84 or any lower limit set by the EIC. OCC Interpretive Letter No. 1122 (July 30, 2009).

–   *Membership in IntercontinentalExchange U.S. Trust (ICE Trust).* A national bank is permitted to become a clearing member of ICE Trust, a clearinghouse for over-the-counter credit default swaps. The bank's exposure to the ICE Trust for the defaults of other members is subject to the lending limit in 12 USC 84 or any lower limit set by the Examiner-in- Charge. Before the bank may become an ICE Trust clearing member, the bank must establish a comprehensive risk management framework to govern the risks associated with its membership, and receive a written supervisory no-objection from its EIC. Other national banks may rely on the letter to become clearing members of ICE Trust, but must obtain prior written EIC approval. OCC Interpretive Letter No. 1113 (March 4, 2009).

–   *Membership in National Securities Clearing Corporation Limited.* Letter concludes that the bank, via its Mumbai branch, may offer clearing services in India, as a custodian clearing member (CCM) of the National Securities Clearing Corporation Limited (NSCCL) where the bank's exposure to the NSCCL for the defaults of other members is subject to the lending limit in 12 USC 84 (Section 84). Before the branch may become an NSCCL CCM, the bank must notify its Examiner-in-Charge (EIC), in writing, of the proposed activities and must receive written notification of the EIC's supervisory no-objection. When a foreign exchange or clearinghouse does not limit a bank's loss exposure to amounts below the section 84 limits, a national bank must comply with the procedures in the attached letter. OCC Interpretive Letter No. 1102 (October 14, 2008).

Other

- **Fixed-Rate, Cumulative Preferred Securities**. A national bank has authority under 12 USC 24 (Seventh), and in accordance with Part 1, to purchase and hold for its own account shares of fixed-rate cumulative preferred securities. The securities have characteristics typically associated with debt instruments, rather than common stock. This conclusion is subject to the condition that the bank will not exercise conversion rights so long as the securities are held by the bank or any subsidiary. OCC Interpretive Letter No. 1086 (August 23, 2007).

- **Municipal Bond Tender Option Certificates**. A national bank may acquire and hold two classes of certificates, one rated investment grade and one unrated, issued by a trust under a tender option bond structure as Type III investment securities, provided the bank can demonstrate that the unrated certificate is the credit equivalent of investment grade. The letter also concludes that the bank also may acquire the certificates under the authority in 12 USC 24(Seventh) to discount and negotiate evidence of debt, subject to the limitations of 12 USC 84 and the requirements of Banking Circular 181 (Rev.). OCC Interpretive Letter No. 1070 (September 6, 2006).

Tying

- **Underwriting Services Conditioned on Bank's Letter of Credit**. A national bank may condition the offering of its securities underwriting services on the use of the bank's letter of credit to secure the bond issue. The traditional bank product exception of 12 USC 1972(1) permits a bank to tie any product or service to a loan, discount, deposit, or trust service offered by that bank. The direct advance of funds to a borrower through a letter of credit is well recognized in the industry as a traditional bank product. OCC Interpretive Letter No. 982 (September 29, 2003).

Technology and Electronic Activities

Digital Certification

- **Digital Certification**. A national bank may act as a certification authority to enable subscribers to generate digital signatures that verify the identity of a sender of an electronic message. Conditional Approval No. 267, reprinted in [1997-1998 Transfer Binder] Fed. Banking L. Rep. (CCH) ¶ 81,256 (January 12, 1998).

- **Multiple Bank Certification Authority Network System**. National banks may invest in a multibank venture to establish an entity that will support a multiple-bank certification authority (CA) network system. The central entity will act as the root CA for the sub-CA banks and will establish business rules, so that customers of any sub-CAs can quickly and easily obtain verification of a certificate issued by any other CA bank in the system. Conditional Approval No. 339 (November 16, 1999).

Electronic Bill Payments

Dispensing Prepaid Alternate Media From ATMs

– *Dispensing Prepaid Alternate Media.* National banks may dispense "alternate media" supplied by merchants, i.e., public transportation tickets, event and attraction tickets, gift certificates, prepaid phone cards, promotional and advertising materials, EBT script, and credit and debit cards, from ATM machines. OCC Interpretive Letter No. 718, reprinted in [1995-1996 Transfer Binder] Fed. Banking L. Rep. (CCH) ¶ 81,033 (March 14, 1996).

Electronic Bill Presentment

– *Electronic Bill Payment.* National banks may invest in an Internet electronic payment system as a complement to existing Internet bill presentment services. The system would also permit customers to make payments not linked to a presented bill. Conditional Approval No. 389, (May 19, 2000).

– *Electronic Bill Payment and Presentment Services Through the Internet.* National banks may have a minority investment in limited liability companies that offer electronic bill payment and presentment services through the Internet. Conditional Approval No. 304 (March 5, 1999).

– *Electronic Interbank Switch.* National banks may invest in an electronic interbank switch to support electronic bill presentment services over the Internet. Conditional Approval No. 332 (October 18, 1999).

Electronic Data Interchange (EDI) Services

– *Minority Interest in EDI Services.* National banks may acquire and hold a minority interest in companies that offer EDI services that allow businesses to send and receive payments, invoices, and orders worldwide. OCC Interpretive Letter No. 732, reprinted in [1995-1996 Transfer Binder] Fed. Banking L. Rep. (CCH) ¶ 81,049 (May 10, 1996).

Electronic Toll Collection

– *Operation of an Electronic Toll Collection System.* National banks may enter a contract with a public authority to operate, on behalf of the public authority, an electronic toll collection system, because the activities involved are part of the business of banking (the collection and remittance of funds and payments) and thus permissible under 12 USC 24(Seventh). OCC Interpretive Letter No. 731, reprinted in [1995-1996 Transfer Binder] Fed. Banking L. Rep. (CCH) ¶ 81,048 (July 1, 1996).

Merchant Processing of Credit Cards via Internet

– *Access to Third-Party Vendors of Services for the Merchant-Processing Industry.* National banks may provide, via Internet links, their merchant- processing customers with information and access to third-party vendors of services for the merchant-processing industry. Corporate Decision No. 99-35 (October 20, 1999).

– *Electronic Transmission of Sales Information Relating to Merchant Processing.* National banks may permit its merchant customers to transmit their sales information over the Internet rather than physically submitting paper sales drafts or electronically transmitting their sales information by a dial terminal. OCC Interpretive Letter (June 27, 1996).

Stored Value

– *Closed Stored Value Card (SVC) Systems.* National banks may invest in LLC that will design, install, and support closed SVC systems at universities and other institutions. OCC Interpretive Letter No 737, reprinted in [1996-1997 Transfer Binder] Fed. Banking L. Rep. (CCH) ¶ 8 1,101 (August 19, 1996).

– *Creation, Sale, and Redemption of Stored Value Cards.* National banks may acquire membership interests in LLCs that operate an "open" stored value card system. This is permissible because the creation, sale, and redemption of electronic stored value in exchange for dollars are part of the business of banking. Conditional Approval No. 220 (December 2, 1996); OCC Interpretive Letter No. 855, reprinted in [1998-1999 Transfer Binder] Fed. Banking L. Rep. (CCH) ¶ 81,312 (March 1, 1999).

– *Participation in a Stored Value Payment System.* A national bank operating subsidiary may invest in a joint venture that will develop and market a stored value system and pursue future opportunities involving stored value. The stored value program will initially focus on payroll distribution for employees without bank accounts, however, the joint venture will also develop and market stored value programs for merchants and others. Conditional Approval No. 568 (December 31, 2002).

– *Sponsoring of a Stored Value System.* A national bank financial subsidiary may engage in a stored value payment system. The national bank may sponsor the stored value systems and associated PIN cards with certain ATM/POS financial networks. The transactions allow for cross border ATM transactions and purchases through deposits in an aggregate account to the benefit of the unbanked public. Conditional Approval No. 568 (December 31, 2002).

Electronic Commerce

• **Advisory Services Regarding Electronic Transactional Services**. A national bank operating subsidiary may provide advisory and consulting services to customers who use the bank's electronic retail or wholesale transactional services; the advice would cover hardware, software, and other technologies necessary to use those services. The subsidiary may also provide advisory and consulting services to business customers on the hardware, software, and other technology necessary to enable those customers to process for themselves banking, economic, and financial information. Corporate Decision No. 2002-11 (June 28, 2002).

- **Collection of Corporate Card Use Data**. A national bank may establish an operating subsidiary that will purchase and then sell or license data processing software that automatically collects information on corporate card use and then merge the data, generate invoices, and approve and make payments. The software also can be licensed to large corporate credit card users. Corporate Decision No. 2003-6 (March 17, 2003).

- **Commercial Web Site Hosting Services**. National banks can host commercially enabled Web sites for small retailers. This service will enable a retailer to operate a Web site that can receive and process credit card orders for its merchandise over the Internet. OCC Interpretive Letter No. 856, reprinted in [1998-1999 Transfer Binder] Fed. Banking L. Rep. (CCH) 181, 313 (March 5, 1999).

- **Computer and Telecommunication Equipment Leasing**. A national bank operating subsidiary may conduct computer and telecommunication equipment leasing activities, including ancillary activities. The ancillary activities include the acquisition of equipment for lease, delivery and installation of leased equipment, sales of off-lease equipment, other occasional sales of equipment, arranging for maintenance contracts, and certain Web site development services. Corporate Decision No. 2002-13 (July 31, 2002).

- **Electronic Marketplace for Nonfinancial Products Over the Internet**. National banks may operate a Web site providing consumers and dealers with detailed information on used cars for sale that meet purchaser preferences. Site may also conduct electronic auctions for dealers. In connection with resulting sales and referrals, the bank will also offer a range of financial products related to vehicle purchases, such as loan and lease arrangements. Corporate Decision No. 97-60 (July 1, 1997).

- **Facilitation of Electronic Commerce Among "Member" Businesses**. A national bank operating subsidiary may support and facilitate electronic commerce by and among a group of "member" businesses by using the Internet to assist member businesses: in transacting business with each other; to refer members to third- party vendors that make products and services available at preferred rates; to enable members to exchange information with each other concerning possible joint activities; to host or support Web sites for members to facilitate their distribution of products and services; to develop and deploy a Web-based payment system for members; and, to deploy systems to track and store financial and transactional information. Incidental to those functions, the Internet site may also provide access to a limited amount of non-financial information that is necessary to attract persons to a virtual small site. Conditional Approval No. 369 (February 25, 2000).

- **Hyperlinks Between Bank Web Sites and Third-Party Sites**. National banks, in the exercise of their finder authority, may establish hyperlinks between their home pages and the Internet pages of third-party providers so that bank customers will be able to access those Web sites from the bank site. Conditional Approval No. 221 (December 3, 1996); Conditional Approval No. 347 (January 29, 2000) (National banks, under their finder authority, can obtain commitments in Web linking agreements with third parties to provide preferential pricing or other terms to bank customers referred to the third party through the bank site).

- **Provision of Electronic Payment Initiation Products**. A national bank may expand the activities of a company in which it holds a noncontrolling interest so that the bank could use the company's certification authority network system to provide electronic payment initiation products to commercial buyers and sellers. These electronic payment initiation products will allow trading parties with no previous trading relationship to complete on-line purchases or trades and simultaneously arrange for payments through their existing banking relationships. The proposed system is a business-to-bank payment initiation service, not an interbank payment system. Corporate Decision No. 2002-4 (February 18, 2002).

- **Services to Internet Merchants**. A national bank may enable small business merchants to acquire a package of electronic services that allows the merchants to create Web stores and process electronic payments for purchases made over the Internet. The national bank, under its authority to act as a finder, can refer the merchants to another unaffiliated company that provides Web site building software and Web hosting services. The bank can provide authorization and processing services necessary for the merchants to accept on-line credit and debit card payments in a secure environment. The bank can also provide the merchants with reports on the activity of their Web stores and answers to "frequently asked questions" on the use of the Web design software based upon answers prepared and supplied by the software company. Finally, the bank also may help other financial institutions to market as finders this package of electronic commerce services to their own merchant customers. Corporate Decision No. 2001-18 (July 3, 2001). See also Corporate Decision No. 2000-08 (June 1, 2000).

- **Trade Finance Facilitation**. A national bank may make a noncontrolling investment in a company that, through its Internet site, facilitates trade financing between exporters and importers by arranging financing, obtaining credit insurance, and acting as escrow and paying agent. Conditional Approval No. 436 (December 19, 2000).

- **Virtual Malls**. National banks may operate a "virtual mall," i.e., a bank-hosted set of Web pages with a collection of links to third-party Web sites organized by product type and available to bank customers, so that they can shop for a range of financial and non-financial products and services via links to sites of third-party vendors and merchants can electronically confirm payment authorization before shipping goods. OCC Interpretive Letter No. 875, reprinted in [Current Transfer Binder] Fed. Banking L. Rep. (CCH) ¶ 81,369 (October 31, 1999).

- **Web Design and Development Services**. National banks, incidental to offering commercially engaged Web site hosting, may provide Web design and development services to their merchant customers. OCC Interpretive Letter No. 875 (October 31, 1999).

Electronic Correspondent Services

- **Electronic Correspondent Services**. A national bank's operating subsidiary may sell computer network services and related hardware to other financial institutions as a correspondent banking service and, thus, part of the business of banking. A subsidiary's sale of full function hardware as part of a package of network services is "incidental" to those correspondent services. OCC Interpretive Letter No. 754, reprinted in [1996-1997 Transfer Binder] Fed. Banking L. Rep. (CCH) 81,118 (November 6, 1996).

Electronic Storage and Safekeeping

- **Electronic Storage and Safekeeping**. As a modern version of national banks' traditional safekeeping function, a national bank may provide an integrated, on- line information service for secure Web-based document storage and retrieval of documents and files containing personal information or valuable confidential trade or business information. Data can be stored on systems controlled by the bank and will be accessible by customers through the Internet or a dedicated line. Except for storage, access, and retrieval, the bank will not process or manipulate the information stored. The bank may also offer its customers the ability to grant third parties controlled access to the stored documents and files so as to enable the use of document collaboration tools. Conditional Approval No. 479 (July 27, 2001).

- **Excess Capacity**. A national bank may use legitimate excess capacity to provide electronic storage and retrieval for external customers (i.e., non-national bank customers). OCC Interpretive Letter No. 888 (March 14, 2000).

Internet Access Service

- **Internet Access Service**. A national bank's operating subsidiary may acquire and hold a minority interest in a limited liability company that supplies a network for home banking systems. Conditional Approval Letter No. 221 (December 4, 1996).

- **Internet Access and Sale of Excess Capacity**. National banks may provide full Internet access service in connection with their Internet banking services and, incidental to that, may sell good faith excess capacity in access service to persons who are not Internet banking customers. OCC Interpretive Letter No. 742, reprinted in [1996-1997 Transfer Binder] Fed. Banking L. Rep. (CCH) ¶ 81,106 (August 19, 1996).

- **Provision of Internet Access to Bank Customers**. A national bank operating subsidiary may provide Internet access to customers in its service area, as an incidental activity to the bank's provision of Internet banking services. Conditional Approval No. 409 (August 10, 2000).

Internet and PC Banking

- **Affinity Marketing via the Internet**. A national bank may solicit "affinity" relationships with other groups and commercial entities to establish a private-label banking clientele. Exercising its authority to use multiple trade names, the bank can offer its products and services to customers or members of the affinity group under a private label through the Internet and establish individual divisions to provide products and services specific to the needs expressed by affinity groups. The bank must comply with OCC guidance with respect to co-brands and private labels. Conditional Approval No. 462 (April 4, 2001).

- **Authentication in an Internet Banking Environment**. Guidance addresses the need for risk-based assessment, customer awareness, and security measures to authenticate customers using a financial institution's Internet-based services. Financial institutions should periodically ensure that their information security program identifies and assesses the risks associated with Internet-based products and services, identifies risk mitigation actions, and measures and evaluates customer awareness efforts; adjust as appropriate their information security program; and implement appropriate risk mitigation strategies. OCC Bulletin 2005-35 (October 12, 2005).

- **Internet Banking Powers**. National banks can offer Internet banking services and, in connection with those activities, provide full Internet access service. OCC Interpretive Letter No. 742, reprinted in [1996-1997 Transfer Binder] Fed. Banking L. Rep. (CCH) ¶ 81,106 (August 19, 1996).

- **Internet Banks**. National banks can deliver products and services to customers primarily through electronic means through a limited-purpose bank. Such banks can operate without any traditional banking offices. In addition to using the mail, customers can conduct their banking transactions by personal computer or by telephoning the automated voice response system or customer service line. Conditional Approval No. 253 (August 20, 1997).

- **Internet Bank, Small Business Focus**. National banks may establish Internet banks that focus on small businesses. Conditional Approval No. 347 (January 29, 2000).

- **Internet Credit Card Banks**. National banks may operate limited-purpose Internet credit card banks. Key features of one such bank include an entirely online credit application and approval process and an Internet direct marketing approach. Conditional Approval No. 312 (May 8, 1999).

- **Internet Full Service Banks**. National banks may be full service Internet banks. Internet-based national bank will not have any traditional banking offices, but will deliver products and services through a variety of electronic delivery channels. Customers will conduct transactions through ATMs, Internet via a transactional Web site, and via a toll-free customer service line. These delivery channels are available at kiosks located on the premises of retail stores for which the bank has a joint marketing arrangement. The bank will operate under a brand name associated with the retail store partner. Conditional Approval No. 313 (July 9, 1999).

- **Mortgage Lending Online**. A national bank may deliver mortgage-lending products online to its retail customers through a variety of electronic delivery channels including the Internet, automated teller machines, and/or remote service units. Conditional Approval No. 462 (April 4, 2001).

- **Provision of Internet-Based Services to Government Agencies**. A national bank may acquire a noncontrolling interest in a LLC that enters into contracts with federal, state, and local government agencies to provide a package of Internet-based services, including development of Web sites, hosting of Web sites, and providing related merchant processing services. OCC Interpretive Letter No. 883 (March 3, 2000).

Software Development, Production, and Licensing

- **Investment in Companies That Develop, Distribute, and Support Software**. National banks may invest and take warrants in companies that develop, distribute, and support software that enables secure payments over the Internet. OCC Interpretive Letter No. 868, reprinted in [Current Transfer Binder] Fed. Banking L. Rep. (CCH) ¶ 81,362 (August 16, 1999).

- **Sale of Web Site Software and Other Web Site Hosting Services**. National bank operating subsidiary may engage in the sale of Web site editing software as part of a bundle of Internet-based Web site hosting services for bank customers. The bank will also use the operating subsidiary to develop new software products to be used by the bank in conjunction with its transaction processing services and in developing its own Internet-based services. Corporate Decision No. 2000-01 (January 29, 2000).

- **Software Development and Production**. National bank may engage in joint ventures to develop and distribute home banking and financial management software to be distributed through the bank and through retail outlets. OCC Interpretive Letter No. 677, reprinted in [1994-1995 Transfer Binder] Fed. Banking L. Rep. (CCH) ¶ 83,625 (June 28, 1995). Sale or License of Corporate Credit Card Data Processing Software. A national bank operating subsidiary may purchase for subsequent sale or license to unaffiliated companies that operate large corporate credit card programs, data processing software designed to monitor corporate credit card usage, merge usage data, generate invoices, and approve/make payments. Corporate Decision No. 2003-6 (March 17, 2003).

COMPLIANCE

Bank Secrecy Act/Anti-Money Laundering

- **Accounts From Foreign Entities**. An interagency advisory provides guidance to institutions concerning the acceptance of accounts from foreign governments, foreign embassies, and foreign political figures. OCC Bulletin 2004-26 (June 16, 2004).

- **Administrative Requests for Suspicious Activity Reports**. In December 2005, the U.S. District Court for the Eastern District of Louisiana held that the OCC's decision denying plaintiff's request for suspicious activity reports (SAR) was unreasonable because the OCC failed to follow its regulations at 12 CF. Part 4 in considering whether plaintiff should be given access to any SARs that may exist. On appeal, the Fifth Circuit vacated the district court's decision ordering release of any SARs that may have been filed, and remanded the case to the district court with instructions that the district court remand the matter to the OCC for initial consideration of the administrative request under the OCC's Touhy regulations. BizCapital Business & Industrial Development Corp. v. Comptroller of the Currency, 406 F.Supp.2d 688 (E.D. La. 2005), reversed in part, 467 F.3d 871 (5th Cir. 2006).

- **Bank Secrecy Act/Anti-Money Laundering Frequently Asked Questions**. This updated set of FAQs provides staff guidance on the application of the rule on Customer Identification Programs for Banks, Savings Associations, Credit Unions and Certain Non-Federally Regulated Banks. OCC Bulletin 2005-16 (April 28, 2005).

- **Customer Identification Program FAQs**. An interagency set of "Frequently Asked Questions" (FAQ) clarifies various aspects of a regulation requiring banks, savings associations, credit unions, and certain non-federally regulated banks to have a customer identification program (CIP). The joint regulation implemented section 326 of the USA PATRIOT Act. OCC Bulletin 2004-3 (January 8, 2004).

- **Denial of Draft Suspicious Activity Report Form Developed by Bank**. The California Court of Appeal ruled on June 17, 2005, that a bank's internal forms used in the process of preparing suspicious activity reports were exempt from discovery to the same extent as the final suspicious activity report. Union Bank of California, N.A. v. Superior Court, 130 Cal.App.4th 378, 29 Cal.Rptr.3d 894 (2005).

- **Denial of Request for Suspicious Activity Reports**. On September 12, 2005, the U.S. District Court for the Northern District of Ohio held that the OCC's decision denying a request for suspicious activity reports (SAR) was reasonable because the BSA's prohibition on the disclosure of a SAR and the OCC's implementing regulation declaring a SAR to be confidential prohibits the disclosure of a SAR to anyone. The court also sustained the constitutionality of the BSA's confidentiality provision and the OCC's implementing regulation. In response to the plaintiff's motion to clarify the decision, the court issued a brief order holding that "SAR- related" documents, defined in the order as documents that could reveal that a SAR was reported, can no more be discovered than the SAR itself. Wuliger v. OCC, 394 F.Supp.2d 1009 (N.D. Ohio 2005).

- **Denial of Request for Suspicious Activity Reports**. Motion to Dismiss filed by OCC in this District Court action to challenge the OCC's decision denying BizCapital's administrative request for access to information about a suspicious activity report (SAR) that may have been filed by a national bank. On December 8, 2005, the Court ruled that the OCC's denial of the request was arbitrary and capricious because the OCC had not weighed BizCapital's need for the document as required by Part 4 in reaching its decision to deny access. On December 23, 2005, the OCC filed a notice of appeal and a motion for a stay of the Court's order of disclosure pending appeal. The motion was granted. BizCapital Business and Industrial Development Corporation v. OCC, F.Supp.2d (E.D. La. 2005) 2005 WL 3543734 (November 23, 2005).

- **Enforcement Guidance**. The OCC provides guidance on its policies for citing violations and taking enforcement actions with respect to the Bank Secrecy Act (BSA) compliance program rule (12 CFR 21.21) and the suspicious activity reporting (SAR) requirements (12 CFR 21.11). OCC Bulletin 2004-51 (November 10, 2004).

- **Safe Harbor for Reports of Suspicious Activities**. The OCC joined other regulatory authorities in issuing interagency guidance on a recent court ruling affirming the statutory safe harbor provision for financial institutions and their employees who report known or suspected criminal offenses or other suspicious activities pursuant to the 1992 Annunzio-Wylie Anti-Money-Laundering Act. "Suspicious Activity Reporting—Interagency Advisory: Federal Court Reaffirms Protections for Financial Institutions Filing Suspicious Activity Reports," OCC Bulletin No. 2004-24 (May 26, 2004).

Consumer

- **Abusive Lending Practices**. Two advisory letters address the avoidance of abusive lending both in a bank's loan originations and in loans acquired through loan brokers or in loan purchase transactions. Guidance outlines the credit, legal, and other risks inherent in predatory lending, and provides detailed recommendations for banks to incorporate in their policies, procedures, and practices in order to minimize those risks. OCC Advisory Letter 2003-02, "Guidelines for National Banks to Guard Against Predatory and Abusive Lending Practices"; OCC Advisory Letter 2003-3, "Avoiding Predatory and Abusive Lending Practices in Brokered and Purchased Loans."

- **Agency Summary Judgment Motion Granted Regarding Challenge to Jointly Issued Consumer Privacy Regulations**. The U.S. District Court for the District of Columbia granted the summary judgment motion filed by the FTC, OCC, Federal Reserve Board, OTS, FDIC, and NCUA. The plaintiffs, who are in the business of selling consumer information, challenged the agencies' joint issuance of bank customer privacy regulations under the Gramm-Leach-Bliley Act as beyond the authority provided for under the act and in violation of plaintiffs' constitutional right to commercial free speech. Specifically at issue was whether the plaintiffs' sale of "credit header" information was subject to the regulations' restrictions and disclosure and reuse. Only one of the plaintiffs, TransUnion, has pursued an appeal before the D.C. Circuit. Individual Reference Services Group, et al. v. FTC, OCC, et al. (D.D.C.) (April 30, 2001).

- **Community Reinvestment Act**. A national bank's contribution to the Louisiana National Guard's Job Challenge Program may be a qualified investment for Community Reinvestment Act (CRA) purposes. The contribution would sponsor a low- or moderate-income local student's participation in the program, a skill- training program that selected students may enter after successful completion of the National Guard's Youth Challenge Program. Such a contribution would have a primary purpose of community development under the CRA rules because it supports a community service targeted to low- and moderate-income individuals, and would benefit the bank's assessment area. OCC Letter (September 11, 2002).

- **Community Reinvestment Act (CRA) Questions and Answers**. The federal financial institution regulatory agencies issued new and revised Interagency Questions and Answers Regarding Community Reinvestment that, among other things, encourage financial institutions to participate in foreclosure prevention programs that have the objective of providing affordable, sustainable, long-term loan restructurings or modifications for homeowners who are facing foreclosure on their primary residences. The questions and answers also address activities undertaken by a majority-owned financial institution in cooperation with a minority- or women-owned financial institution or a low-income credit union. 74 *Federal Register* 498 (January 6, 2009).

- **Credit Card Marketing Practices**. Certain practices may entail unfair or deceptive acts or practices and may expose a bank to compliance and reputation risks. These include credit card solicitations that advertise credit limits "up to" a maximum dollar amount, when that credit limit is, in fact, seldom extended; the practice of using promotional rates in credit card solicitations without clearly disclosing the significant restrictions on the applicability of those rates; and increasing a cardholder's annual percentage rate or otherwise increasing a cardholder's cost of credit when the circumstances triggering the increase, or the creditor's right to effectuate the increase, have not been disclosed fully or prominently. OCC Advisory Letter 2004-80 "Credit Card Practices" (September 14, 2004).

- **Disclosure of Customer Account Number to Insurance Marketer**. Under Gramm-Leach-Bliley Act (GLBA) privacy rules, financial institutions may not disclose customer account numbers to a marketer of insurance products, even if the customer has consented to such disclosure. As a general rule, GLBA prohibits the disclosure of account numbers to nonaffiliated third parties for use in marketing. This prohibition remains effective after the customer has accepted the offer to buy the product being sold. OCC Interpretive Letter No. 910 (May 25, 2001).

- **Electronic Delivery of Consumer Disclosures**. The Electronic Signatures in Global and National Commerce Act (E-SIGN Act) permits disclosures to be made or delivered electronically, provided that the consumer consents to such disclosures in accordance with the requirements of the act. National banks contemplating making disclosures to their retail customers by electronic means should determine whether the special consumer consent provisions of the act apply to those disclosures. This advisory encourages national banks to pay particular attention to several issues when obtaining effective consumer consent to electronic disclosures. OCC Advisory Letter 2004-11 "Electronic Consumer Disclosures and Notices" (October 1, 2004).

- **Enforcement of the Federal Trade Commission Act**. The Rhode Island Supreme Court, affirming the court below, held that the OCC had authority under the Federal Trade Commission Act to take enforcement action against national banks for unfair and deceptive practices, which prevents private plaintiffs from bringing an action against the bank under the Rhode Island Deceptive Trade Practices Act. Chavers v. Fleet Bank (R.I.), No. 02-201 (Rh.Isl. Sup. Ct., February 26, 2004).).

- **Frequently Asked Questions on Identity Theft Rules**. Six federal agencies issued a set of frequently asked questions and answers (FAQ) to help financial institutions, creditors, users of consumer reports, and issuers of credit cards and debit cards comply with federal regulations on identity theft and address discrepancies. The FAQs provide guidance on numerous aspects of the rules on identity theft "red flags" and notices of address discrepancies, which implement sections of the Fair and Accurate Credit Transactions Act of 2003 (FACT Act). These rules were issued jointly on November 9, 2007, including information on which types of entities and accounts are covered, establishment and administration of an Identity Theft Prevention Program, addressing validation requirements applicable to card issuers, and the obligations of users of consumer reports upon receiving a notice of address discrepancy. OCC Joint News Release 2009-65 (June 11, 2009)

- **Gift Card Disclosures**. OCC guidance to national banks and examiners on disclosure and marketing issues associated with gift cards focuses on the need for national banks that issue gift cards to do so in a manner in which both purchasers and recipients are fully informed of the product's terms and conditions. National banks that issue gift cards should take appropriate steps to ensure that consumers are fully informed about the material terms and conditions of these products, noting that gift cards present special challenges because providing disclosures to a purchaser may not suffice to inform the gift card recipient about the product. OCC Bulletin No. 2006-34 (August 14, 2006).

- **Guidance on Response Programs for Unauthorized Access to Customer Information and Customer Notice. (12 CFR 30)**. The OCC, the FRB, the FDIC, and the OTS issued an interpretation of section 501(b) of the Gramm-Leach- Bliley Act and the Interagency Guidelines Establishing Standards for Safeguarding Customer Information. The interpretation describes the agencies' expectations regarding the response programs, including customer notification procedures, that a financial institution should develop and implement to address the unauthorized access to, or use of, customer information that could result in substantial harm or inconvenience to a customer. Federal Reserve, 70 Federal Register 15736 (March 29, 2005).

- **Guidance on Risk Mitigation and Response to Web Site Spoofing Incidents**. Web-site spoofing is a method of creating fraudulent Web sites that look similar, if not identical to an actual site, such as that of a bank, with the goal of enticing customers to reveal information that would enable a criminal to use customers' accounts to commit fraud or steal the customers' identities. In response to the growing incidents of Web-site spoofing, the OCC issued guidance to banks on how to respond to such incidents and steps that they can take to mitigate the risks to themselves and their customers from such incidents. OCC Bulletin No. 2005-24 (July 1, 2005).

- **HMDA Data**. A set of frequently asked questions that addresses Home Mortgage Disclosure Act (HMDA) new loan price data disclosed in 2005. OCC Bulletin No. 2005-17 (May 2, 2005).

- **Illustrations of Consumer Information for Hybrid Adjustable Rate Mortgage Products**. Interagency guidance designed to illustrate the type of information to be provided to consumers on hybrid adjustable rate mortgage products, as contemplated in the interagency Statement on Subprime Mortgage Lending 72 *Federal Register* 37569 (July 10, 2007), including information about potential payment shock. The guidance sets out four illustrations consisting of 1) a narrative explanation of adjustable rate mortgage products (ARM) with a reduced initial interest rate, and 2) three separate charts comparing such ARMs with fixed rate mortgage products. 73 *Federal Register* 30997 (May 29, 2008).

- **Model Privacy Notice Form**. Federal regulatory agencies issued a final model privacy notice form to make it easier for consumers to understand how financial institutions collect and share information about consumers. Under the Gramm- Leach-Bliley Act (GLB Act), institutions must notify consumers of their information-sharing practices and inform consumers of their right to opt out of certain sharing practices. The Financial Services Regulatory Relief Act of 2006 amended the GLB Act to require the agencies to propose a succinct, easy-to-read, and comprehensible model form that allows consumers to easily compare the privacy practices of different financial institutions. The model form can be used by financial institutions to comply with these requirements. The final rule provides that a financial institution that chooses to use the model form obtains a "safe harbor" and will satisfy the disclosure requirements for notices. The rule also removes, after a transition period, the sample clauses now included in the appendices of the agencies' privacy rules. 74 *Federal Register* 62890 (December 1, 2009).

- **Nontraditional Mortgage Products**. Interagency guidance addresses both safety and soundness and consumer protection issues raised by interest-only and payment option mortgage loans. The consumer protection portion of the guidance states that institutions should take appropriate steps to alert consumers to the risks of these products, including the likelihood of increased future payment obligations and the risk of negative amortization, when consumers are shopping for a mortgage. The guidance also provides disclosure recommendations and describes practices that institutions should avoid. OCC Bulletin No. 2006-42 (October 4, 2006).

- **OCC Guidelines Establishing Standards for Residential Mortgage Lending Practices. (12 CFR 30).** Final guidelines concerning the residential mortgage lending practices of national banks and their operating subsidiaries protect against national bank involvement in predatory, abusive, unfair, or deceptive residential mortgage lending practices. The guidelines identify practices that are consistent with sound residential mortgage lending practices and describe terms and practices that may lead to predatory, abusive, unfair, or deceptive lending practices. They also address steps banks should take to mitigate risks associated with their purchase of residential mortgage loans and use of mortgage brokers to originate loans. 70 *Federal Register* 6329 (February 7, 2005).

- **Obtaining Credit Reports in Business Loan Transactions.** Under the Fair Credit Reporting Act (FCRA), lenders need not obtain a consumer's consent before obtaining the consumer's credit report in connection with a business credit transaction where the individual is or will be personally liable on the loan, such as in the case of an individual proprietor, co-signer, or guarantor. The FCRA permits the furnishing of consumer reports to persons who intend to use them in connection with extensions of credit to the consumer, and this criterion is satisfied where the consumer may be liable on the loan. Interagency Letter (May 31, 2001). See also OCC Advisory Letter 2001-6 "Fair Credit Reporting Act" (July 6, 2001).

- **OCC Consumer Tips for Avoiding Foreclosure Rescue Scams.** OCC issuance identifying common types of foreclosure rescue schemes, providing guidance on steps consumers can take to protect themselves from such schemes, and setting forth information about how consumers can obtain legitimate assistance in helping to address their financial problems. OCC Consumer Advisory 2008-1 (May 16, 2008).

- **Overdraft Programs.** Certain overdraft programs, offered by third-party vendors and designed primarily to increase banks' fee income, raise legal, supervisory, and policy concerns. Supervisory concerns arise from the potential credit risk created by the overdraft loans and the bank's arrangements with the third-party vendor providing the product. Policy concerns arise because the programs may encourage customers to write "not sufficient funds" checks, thus promoting poor fiscal responsibility on the part of some consumers. These programs also may raise potential issues under the Truth in Lending Act, Truth in Savings Act, Electronic Fund Transfer Act, Equal Credit Opportunity Act, Federal Trade Commission Act, and Regulation O. OCC Interpretive Letter No. 914 (August 3, 2001).

- **Overdraft Protection Programs Guidance.** The guidance describes federal consumer compliance laws that may apply to overdraft protection programs, and industry best practices for the marketing and communications of these programs. Such practices include clearly disclosing fees, explaining the impact of transaction clearing policies on the overdraft fees consumers may incur, disclosing the types of consumer banking transactions covered by the program, and monitoring program usage. The agencies also advised financial institutions to alert consumers before a transaction triggers any fees; to provide consumers the opportunity either to opt-in or opt-out of the program; and to notify consumers promptly each time overdraft protection is used. 70 *Federal Register* 9127 (February 24, 2005).

- **Placing Loan Account Numbers on Mortgage-Related Documents**. Under the GLBA privacy rules, lenders may place the borrower's loan account number on mortgages, deeds of trust, and assignments and releases of mortgages that are then recorded in public records. This practice is not prohibited by GLBA's provisions on disclosing account numbers, which, as a general rule, ban the disclosure of account numbers to nonaffiliated third parties for use in marketing. In addition, this practice falls within the exception to GLBA's opt-out requirements for disclosures of information that are "necessary to effect, administer, or enforce the transaction" as that term is defined in GLBA. OCC Interpretive Letters Nos. 917 and 918 (September 4, 2001).

- **School-Based Savings Programs**. The OCC encourages national bank participation in financial literacy initiatives such as school-based bank savings programs, which can qualify for positive consideration under Community Reinvestment Act requirements. "School-Based Bank Savings Programs: Bringing Financial Education to Students," Community Developments Insights (April 2009).

- **Secured Credit Cards**. National banks should not offer secured credit card products (or similar unsecured products) in which security deposits (or fees) are charged to the credit card account if that practice will substantially reduce the amount of available credit and card utility for the consumer. The OCC enumerates recommended practices for issuers of secured credit cards in such areas as product marketing, product structure and terms, and credit risk management. OCC Advisory Letter 2004-4 (April 28, 2004).

- **Servicemembers Civil Relief Act: Legal Requirements**. OCC issuance provided general information about the provisions of the Servicemembers Civil Relief Act (SCRA) that are most likely to affect national banks. The issuance also discussed revisions to the SCRA made by the Housing and Economic Recovery Act of 2008 that provide additional protections to servicemembers by extending the periods during which certain provisions apply. OCC Bulletin 2008-30 (October 24, 2008).

- **Unfair or Deceptive Acts or Practices**. In evaluating whether a national bank or its operating subsidiary has engaged in unfair or deceptive acts or practices, the OCC will utilize the legal standards that have been developed under the Federal Trade Commission Act. Potentially unfair or deceptive acts or practices also may raise issues under the Truth in Lending Act, the Equal Credit Opportunity Act, and other laws. National banks and their operating subsidiaries should take affirmative steps to avoid the legal and reputation risks that would ensue from engaging in unfair or deceptive acts or practices. OCC Advisory Letter 2002-3 "Guidance on Unfair or Deceptive Acts or Practices" (March 22, 2002).

- **Writing a Check: Understanding Your Rights**. Consumer advisory provides consumers with important information about their rights when they use checks to make payments. The advisory outlines the different ways that checks can be processed and the significance for consumers of those differences. For example, the advisory informs consumers that various methods for electronic check processing may mean that funds are taken from consumers' bank accounts more quickly than before. As a result, it is even more important for consumers to ensure that they have enough money in their accounts to cover checks at the time they write them. The advisory also discusses the different laws and regulations governing check transactions, how consumers' rights may vary depending on how a check is processed, and how consumers may resolve problems in connection with their checks. OCC Consumer Advisory 2005-1(August 2, 2005), OCC News Release 2005-75 (August 2, 2005).

INVESTMENTS[1]

- **Acquisition of Preferred Securities**. A national bank may purchase and hold the preferred securities of two special-purpose entities that hold interests in Australian mortgage assets. OCC Interpretive Letter No. 1027 (May 3, 2005).

- **Acquisition of Preferred Stock of an Unaffiliated Company**. A national bank has authority to acquire and hold the preferred stock of an unaffiliated company, pursuant to its authority to discount and negotiate evidences of debt, where the preferred stock is in substance a debt obligation of the issuer. The bank acquired the preferred stock as partial consideration for the disposition of a loan portfolio to the company. The bank's existing holdings represent less than 5 percent of the bank's capital and surplus and are within applicable prudential standards and regulatory limits. OCC Interpretive Letter No. 941 (June 11, 2002).

- **Agricultural Cooperative**. Under Part 24, a national bank may purchase common stock in an agricultural cooperative, where the bank's liability was limited to the amount of its equity investment. The cooperative was initiated by a local economic development authority and local farmers and businesses as a way to promote the economic development of the area, and had received financial support from both the economic development authority and the federal government. The cooperative also benefited low- and moderate-income individuals by creating permanent jobs for those individuals. Approval Letter (September 4, 2001), National Bank Community Development Investments 2001 Directory.

- **Agricultural Credit Corporations**. National banks may purchase stock of a corporation organized to make loans to farmers and ranchers for agricultural purposes. An investment in such an agricultural credit corporation may not exceed 20 percent of a national bank's capital and surplus, unless the national bank owns at least 80 percent. 12 USC 24(Seventh).

---

[1] For investments in partnerships, note that subsidiaries of national banks may become general partners, but national banks may not.

- **Asset-Backed Securities**. National banks may invest up to 25 percent of capital and surplus in marketable investment grade securities that are fully secured by interests in a pool of loans to numerous obligors and in which a national bank may invest directly. 12 CFR 1.2(m), 1.3(f).

- **Banker's Acceptances**. National banks may invest in banker's acceptances created by other nonaffiliated banks without limit, if they are created in accordance with 12 USC 372, and are thus "eligible" for discount with a Federal Reserve bank. But section 372(b), (c), and (d) restrict investment in the aggregate amount of the banker's acceptances created by any one bank. Holdings of "ineligible" banker's acceptances must be included in the purchasing bank's lending limit to the accepting bank. 12 USC 84; 12 CFR. 32.

- **Banker's Banks**. National banks may invest in banker's banks, or their holding companies, in an amount up to 10 percent of the national bank's capital stock and unimpaired surplus. In addition, national banks may not hold more than 5 percent of the voting securities of a banker's bank or holding company. 12 USC 24(Seventh). A banker's bank may be organized as a national bank, and the OCC may waive requirements that are applicable to national banks in general if they are inappropriate for a banker's bank and would impede the provision of its services. 12 USC 27(b); 12 CFR 5.20.

- **Bank-Owned Life Insurance (BOLI)**. A national bank's investment in separate-account bank-owned life insurance will be considered a qualified investment under the Community Reinvestment Act (CRA) if the separate account in which the bank invests is comprised of investments intended to be qualified under the CRA. OCC Interpretive Letter No. 1008 (July 19, 2004).

- **Bank's Own Stock**. National banks may purchase treasury stock to fulfill a legitimate corporate purpose, including in connection with an employee stock purchase plan, directors qualifying shares, or a reverse stock split. 12 USC 83; OCC Interpretive Letter No. 825, reprinted in [1997-1998 Transfer Binder] Fed. Banking L. Rep. (CCH) ¶ 81,274 (March 16, 1998); OCC Interpretive Letter No. 786, reprinted in [1997 Transfer Binder] Fed. Banking L. Rep. (CCH) ¶ 81,213 (June 9, 1997); OCC Interpretive Letter No. 660, reprinted in [1994-1995 Transfer Binder] Fed. Banking L. Rep. (CCH) ¶ 83,608 (December 19, 1994). National banks may make loans on the security of their own shares pursuant to 12 USC 83 and 12 CFR 7.2019.

- **Bank Premises**. National banks may invest in bank premises without OCC approval, if 1) the aggregate amount of the investment is less than or equal to the national bank's capital stock; or 2) the aggregate amount of the investment is less than or equal to 150 percent of the national bank's capital and surplus, and the national bank is well capitalized and has a CAMEL rating of 1 or 2, provided that the bank provides the OCC notice 30 days after this investment. Prior OCC approval is required for investments in bank premises that do not meet the above criteria, but the application may be deemed approved after 30 days, unless the OCC notifies the bank otherwise. 12 USC 29, 371d; 12 CFR 5.37, 7.1000; Conditional Approval No. 298 (December 15, 1998).

- *Bank Premises*. A national bank may hold, as permissible bank premises, commercial facilities with lodging for out-of-town bank visitors. The bank may make excess space available to the general public. OCC Interpretive Letter No. 1045 (December 5, 2005).

- *Bank Premises*. A national bank may hold, as permissible bank premises, a building that consists of both office space and commercial facilities for lodging out-of-town bank visitors. The bank may make excess space available to the general public and, in order to make the building financially feasible, may develop and sell residential condominiums on four floors. OCC Interpretive Letter No. 1044 (December 5, 2005).

- *Bank Premises*. A national bank may construct a new office complex on existing bank premises and lease unused space as excess bank premises. OCC Interpretive Letter No. 1034 (April 1, 2005).

- *Bank Premises*. A national bank may lease a portion of parkland, held as bank premises, to third party. OCC Interpretive Letter No. 758 (April 5, 1996).

- *Bank Premises*. A national bank may add space to two existing bank buildings and lease all new space to third parties. OCC Interpretive Letter (March 10, 1994), available in Lexis-Nexis.

- *Bank Premises*. A national bank may lease condominium, used for out-of- area bank visitors, to third parties when not in use by bank visitors. OCC Interpretive Letter No. 1043 (July 8, 1993).

- *Bank Premises*. A national bank may license use of space on its premises to a third party. OCC Interpretive Letter No. 630 (May 11, 1993).

- *Bank Premises*. A national bank may hold condominium for use of out-of- area visitors. OCC Interpretive Letter No. 1042 (January 21, 1993).

- *Bank Premises*. A national bank may purchase building to house its retail brokerage business, and lease building to third-party broker that will have dual employees with the bank. OCC Interpretive Letter (June 24, 1992), available in Lexis-Nexis.

- *Bank Premises*. A national bank may lease portion of storage facility on bank premises to unrelated third party. OCC Interpretive Letter (December 16, 1991), available in Lexis-Nexis.

- *Bank Premises*. A national bank authorized to develop portion of new bank premises building as office condominium and sell the condominiums. OCC Interpretive Letter (August 14, 1985), available in Lexis-Nexis.

- *Bank Premises*. A national bank may lease lobby space to variety of third parties. OCC Interpretive Letter No. 274 (December 2, 1983).

– *Bank Premises*. A national bank may own apartment in Los Angeles for use by its CEO who maintains his primary residence elsewhere. OCC Interpretive Letter No. 2 (December 13, 1977).

– *Bank Premises*. A national bank may occupy percentage of office complex and lease remaining space to third parties. Wirtz v. First National Bank & Trust Co., 365 F.2.d 641 (10th Cir. 1966) (August 30, 1966).

– *Bank Premises*. A national bank has authority to tear down bank building and construct new six-story office building in which bank will occupy only first floor, and lease excess space to third parties. Wingert v. First National Bank, 175 F. 739 (4th Cir. 1909), appeal dismissed, 223 U.S. 670, 672 (1912) (December 16, 1909).

– *Bank Premises*. The National Bank Act does not preclude a national bank, acting in good faith, from maximizing the utility of its banking premises by leasing excess bank premises to third parties. Brown v. Schleier, 118 F. 981 (8th Cir. 1902), aff'd, 194 U.S. 18 (1904) (November 10, 1902).

- **Bank Service Companies**. National banks may invest in bank service companies if the amount invested does not exceed 10 percent of the bank's capital and surplus and all investments in bank service companies do not exceed 5 percent of the national bank's assets. 12 USC 1862; 12 CFR 5.35.

- **Business Trusts**. National banks may acquire certificates of participation in business trusts created to hold and manage a substantial portion of the bank's investment securities portfolio. OCC Interpretive Letter No. 745, reprinted in [Current Transfer Binder] Fed. Banking L. Rep. (CCH) ¶ 81,110 (August 27, 1996).

- **CD Investments Up to 10 Percent Investment Limit**. In connection with a request for prior approval of an affordable housing investment, the OCC approved a national bank's request to self-certify future affordable, community development (CD) housing investments that would exceed 5 percent of its capital and surplus, up to a maximum of 10 percent of capital and surplus. The requirements of 12 CFR 24 relating to self-certification and all other requirements of the regulation will apply to the additional investments. Approval Letter (August 1, 2001), National Bank Community Development Investments 2001 Directory.

- **Certificates of a U.S. Agency Created Under the Foreign Assistance Act**. Certificates issued by a U.S. agency created under the Foreign Assistance Act may qualify as Type I securities under 12 CFR Part 1 and accordingly are available for investment by national banks without limitation, subject to safety and soundness considerations. OCC Interpretive Letter No. 1001 (May 3, 2004).

- **Clearinghouse**. In a reorganization of the clearinghouse into a holding company with subsidiaries, national banks may lawfully acquire and hold minority interests in both the new holding company and its subsidiaries. OCC Interpretive Letter No. 993 (May 16, 2004).

- **Closed-End Mutual Fund**. National bank may purchase an equity interest in a closed-end mutual fund that finances affordable housing primarily for low- and moderate-income individuals. The fund is structured as a Business Development Company under the Investment Company Act of 1940. The fund purchases securities backed by loans to homebuyers with incomes below 80 percent of median income as well as loans to sponsors of multifamily housing units that use federal low-income housing tax credits or financing provided by HUD. The fund also invests in HUD-guaranteed securities that support community development in low-income areas. Approval of Bank's Self-Certification (April 20, 2001), National Bank Community Development Investments 2001 Directory.

- **Collateralized Bond Obligations**. National banks may purchase marketable, investment-grade collateralized bond obligations as Type III investments, even though certain of the underlying assets are not investment grade. Letter from Tena Alexander, Senior Attorney, dated August 3, 1999.

- **Collateralized Mortgage Obligations (CMO)**. National banks may purchase CMOs, which may be classified as Type I, IV, or V securities under 12 CFR 1.

- **Commercial Mortgage-Related Securities**. National banks may invest in certain commercial mortgage-backed securities. 12 USC 24(Seventh); 12 CFR 1.2(l).

- **Commercial Paper (i.e., Short-Term, Unsecured Promissory Notes Usually Issued by Companies to Meet Their Immediate Cash Needs)**. National banks may hold commercial paper as loans, subject to the lending limits and loan underwriting safety and soundness standards. 12 USC 24(Seventh) and 84; 12 CFR 1 and 32. National banks may issue commercial paper. OCC Interpretive Letter No. (May 4, 1973).

- **Community Development Entity Purchasing, Constructing, and Operating an Ethanol Plant**. Under 12 USC 24(Eleventh), a national bank may make an investment in a community and economic development entity that will purchase, construct, and operate an ethanol plant that is located in a low- and moderate- income (LMI) geography and will provide jobs to unskilled individuals. Community Development Investment Letter 2005-3 (July 20, 2005).

- **Community Reinvestment Act; Employment Fund**. A national bank's proposed investment in a fund with the purpose of providing employment for low- and moderate-income individuals would be a qualified investment under the Community Reinvestment Act regulations. The fund's sole purpose is to invest in a limited liability company that will employ individuals the majority of whom will be in the low- and moderate-income categories, and who will be expected to qualify for various federal employment tax credits. The bank's investment will finance the hiring of employees who will perform various types of work, including clerical, retail, security, and building maintenance. The bank's investment will also help to finance the provision of ancillary services to facilitate employees' continued employment, such as job training, medical insurance, and employee assistance programs. OCC Interpretive Letter No. 983 (October 24, 2003).

- **Community Reinvestment Act; New Market Tax Credits**. A national bank's investment in connection with the New Markets Tax Credit program in a "Community Development Entity" (CDE), or a loan by a bank's CDE to a "Qualified Active Low-Income Community Business" or to another CDE, would receive consideration as a qualified investment or a community development loan, respectively, under the Community Reinvestment Act regulations. OCC Interpretive Letter No. 984 (December 17, 2003).

- **Connecticut Housing Finance Authority Bonds**. A national bank may purchase Connecticut Housing Finance Authority Bonds as Type I securities. They are subject to a 20 percent risk-weight under the OCC's risk-based capital regulation. OCC Interpretive Letter No. 907 (February 1, 2001).

- **Consolidation of Public Welfare Investments Into CDC**. A national bank may consolidate its public welfare investment activities in an existing community development corporation (CDC). The CDC would manage its portfolio so that the majority of its investments qualify as public welfare investment under 12 CFR 24. Thus, the CDC would be primarily engaged in making public welfare investment, and the bank's investments in the CDC would be designed primarily to promote the public welfare, as required by 12 USC 24(Eleventh). Approval Letter (February 14, 2000).

- **Convertible Bonds**. A federal branch's purchases of bonds convertible into equity are permissible investments under Part 1 if the bonds are the credit equivalent of investment grade and marketable. A national bank may purchase bonds convertible into equity where it does not exercise the conversion feature. OCC Interpretive Letter No. 930 (March 11, 2002).

- **Convertible Securities**. National banks may purchase securities convertible into stock, provided that convertibility is not at the option of the issuer. 12 CFR 1.6.

- **Corporate Debt Securities.** National banks may invest in any corporate debt security, provided the securities are marketable debt obligations that are not predominantly speculative in nature and total investments in any one issuer do not exceed 10 percent of the national bank's capital and surplus. 12 USC 24(Seventh); 12 CFR 1.

- **Corporations That Sell or Lease Check Cashing Machines**. National banks can hold a minority investment in a corporation that sells and leases check-cashing machines to third parties. Conditional Approval No. 307 (March 19, 1999).

- **Crime Prevention Programs in Nursing Homes**. A national bank may purchase preferred stock in a foundation that operates crime prevention programs in nursing homes. The foundation uses the bank's funds to purchase government and agency securities. Interest earned on these securities is used to fund crime prevention activities in nursing homes located in low- and moderate-income areas or occupied by low- and moderate-income residents. Community Development Investment Letter 2003-4 (November 17, 2003).

- **Debt Rating Requirement for Establishing Financial Subsidiaries**. A national bank may rely on the rating assigned to the uninsured portion of the bank's certificates of deposit to satisfy the debt rating requirement necessary to establish a financial subsidiary under Section 121 of the Gramm-Leach-Bliley Act. The certificates of deposit qualify as "eligible debt" for purposes of the requirement under Section 121 that any of the 50 largest insured banks must have at least one investment grade rated issue of debt outstanding in order for the bank to establish a financial subsidiary. OCC Interpretive Letter No. 981 (August 14, 2003).

- **Delinquent Real Estate Tax Liens**. National banks may invest in delinquent real estate tax liens, where state law does not consider such liens to represent interests in real property. OCC Interpretive Letter No. 717, reprinted in [1995-1996 Transfer Binder] Fed. Banking L. Rep. (CCH) ¶ 81,032 (March 22, 1996).

- **Deposit Accounts**. National banks also may make deposits in other depository institutions, provided that total deposits in any nonmember bank do not exceed 10 percent of the national bank's capital and surplus. 12 USC 463. National banks may purchase notes issued by another bank, affiliate, or bank holding company. OCC Interpretive Letter (October 12, 1970).

- **DPC Stock**. National banks may hold securities acquired through foreclosure or otherwise in the ordinary course of collecting a debt previously contracted (DPC). Such securities may be held five years, unless the OCC extends the holding period for up to another five years. 12 USC 24(Seventh) (incidental powers clause); OCC Interpretive Letter No. 643, reprinted in Fed. Banking L. Rep. (CCH) ¶ 83, 551 (July 1, 1992); OCC Interpretive Letter No. 511, reprinted in [1990-1991 Transfer Binder] Fed. Banking L. Rep. (CCH) ¶ 83,213 (June 20, 1990).

- **Environmental Redevelopment Fund**. National bank may purchase member shares in a limited liability company (LLC) that primarily benefits low- and moderate- income areas. The LLC provides financing to private and public sector borrowers for environmental analysis and remediation of properties with environmental contamination issues for reuse to attract new and growing businesses, create jobs, provide affordable housing, and support other community development efforts. In addition to the LLC structure, the fund would also seek to protect investors by obtaining third-party insurance for projects that have residual risk, as well as pooled insurance for its portfolio. Approval of Bank's Self-Certification (July 18, 2001) National Bank Community Development Investments 2001 Directory.

- **Equity or Below-Investment-Grade Debt in Exchange for Corporate Debt**. A national bank may accept, as part of a court-administered bankruptcy proceeding, equity or below-investment-grade debt in exchange for corporate debt originally acquired and held as a Type III investment security, under the authority of national banks to accept such securities in satisfaction of debts previously contracted. OCC Interpretive Letter No. 1007 (September 7, 2004).

- **Fannie Mae and Freddie Mac Perpetual Preferred Stock**. A national bank may invest in perpetual preferred stock issued by Fannie Mae and Freddie Mac without limit, subject to safety and soundness considerations. OCC Interpretive Letter No. 931 (March 15, 2002).

- **Federal Employment Tax Credits**. A national bank may purchase an equity interest in a limited liability company (LLC) whose primary purpose is to invest in an operating company that employs individuals, which employment is expected to qualify the operating for federal employment tax credits, including the Work Opportunity Credit, the Welfare to Work Credit, and the Renewal Community Employment Credit. The bank represented that most of the individuals will be low- and moderate-income individuals, and some may reside in low- and moderate-income areas and/or in areas that have been targeted for redevelopment by the federal government as renewal communities. The LLC will assign the individuals to provide labor hours with companies, many of which operate in low- and moderate-income areas or in areas that have been targeted for redevelopment by a government agency. In addition, the LLC will provide job training, medical insurance, and employee assistance programs for its employees. Community Development Investment Letter 2003-1 (September 26, 2003).

- **Financial Services Company Generating an Enhanced Yield Based on Foreign Tax Benefits**. A national bank operating subsidiary may invest in the preferred shares of a foreign domiciled company. A foreign domiciled bank will be the only other co-investor in the company. The foreign company will invest in long-term assets of the national bank and extend long term credit to the foreign bank co-investor. The structure of the transactions achieves for the company certain foreign tax benefits, which ultimately accrue to its investors. Conditional Approval No. 595 (June 5, 2003).

- **Financing Source for Charter School Facilities**. A national bank may invest in a financing source for charter school facilities when the funds will be made available to charter schools in the mid-Atlantic region that enroll students from predominantly low-income households or are located in predominantly low-income neighborhoods. Community Development Investment Letter 2005-2 (April 13, 2005).

- **Fixed Rate Annuities**. Fixed rate annuities purchased by a national bank are, in substance, debt obligations of the issuing insurance company. OCC Interpretive Letter No. 1021 (February 17, 2005).

- **Foreign Operating Subsidiary**. A national bank and a foreign bank may jointly own a foreign entity that will hold, purchase, and sell loans and other extensions of credit. Although the national bank owns only 10 percent of the voting rights, the entity qualifies as an operating subsidiary of the national bank because the national bank may exercise control over it. Conditional Approval No. 646 (June 28, 2004).

- **Foreign Government Securities**. National banks may deal in, underwrite, or invest in securities of Canada and political subdivisions of Canada. 12 USC 24(Seventh); 12 CFR 1.2(i). National banks may also invest in the securities of other foreign governments, provided that the securities are marketable debt obligations that are not predominantly speculative in nature and no more than 10 percent of a national bank's capital and surplus is invested in the securities of any one foreign government. 12 CFR 1.2(e), (j).

- **Foundation**. A national bank may make an investment in a foundation that will use the funds to help capitalize a loan pool that makes loans that support affordable housing, community services, or permanent jobs for low- and moderate-income individuals, financing for small businesses; area revitalization or stabilization; or other activities, services or facilities that primarily promote the public welfare. The foundation is a community development financial institution certified by the U.S. Department of the Treasury. Community Development Letter 2003-2 (April 6, 2003).

- **Fund to Acquire Limited Partnership Interests in Native American Affordable Housing**. A national bank may made an investment in a fund created to acquire limited partnership interests in affordable rental housing properties that are located on, or near Native American reservations in Arizona, Wisconsin, Minnesota, Montana, North Dakota, South Dakota, and Wyoming. The fund's projects qualify for federal low-income housing tax credits and historic rehabilitation tax credits and primarily target low- and moderate-income persons and families. Each project is sponsored by an Indian tribe, an affiliated Tribal housing association, Indian housing authority, Indian tribally designated housing entity, Indian nonprofit housing corporation, or similar tribal entity. Approval Letter (April 10, 2000).

- **Gold Shares**. A national bank may buy and sell, for its own account, exchange- traded units of beneficial interest in gold. OCC Interpretive Letter No. 1013 (January 7, 2005).

- **Hedging DPC Stock**. A national bank may purchase and hold options on the shares of stock of a company when the bank has acquired shares of that company in satisfaction of debts previously contracted (DPC). The bank would hold the options to hedge the market risk associated with changes in the value of the DPC shares. OCC Interpretive Letter No. 961 (March 17, 2003).

- **Historic Tax Credit Investment**. National banks may invest in historic tax credit investment in the Central Vermont Arts Center Limited Partnership. The partnership will finance the renovation of a vacant historic property located in an economic revitalization area in Barre City, Vermont. The general partner and project sponsor is a nonprofit corporation that will also lease space for artists and operate an art gallery and teaching facility. The facility will support the establishment of small businesses by providing artists and artisans with studio space and an opportunity to market their work. The proposal was consistent with 12 CFR 24 because the project was intended to serve as the cornerstone for renewed small business investment and area revitalization, and the property was located in an area that the local government had targeted for revitalization. Approval Letter (October 19, 2000).

- **Housing Investments**. National banks may invest in various HUD-insured loans and obligations issued by government housing projects. National banks may also invest in state housing corporations, subject to a limit of 5 percent of the national bank's capital stock paid and unimpaired plus 5 percent of its unimpaired surplus fund. 12 USC 24(Seventh).

- **Insurance Company Products and Investment Funds, Hedging**. National bank subsidiaries may hold various insurance company products and investment funds containing bank-ineligible securities to hedge, on a dollar-for-dollar basis, the subsidiary's obligations to make payments to employees under certain deferred compensation plans. OCC Interpretive Letter No. 878, reprinted in [Current Transfer Binder] Fed. Banking L. Rep. (CCH) ¶ 81-375 (December 22, 1999).

- **Insurance, Investment in Company That Provides Marketing and Consulting Services to Insurance Agencies**. National bank's insurance agency subsidiaries may acquire a minority interest in a company that provides marketing and consulting services to insurance agencies. Conditional Approval No. 302 (January 21, 1999).

- **Insurance, Investment in Title Agency**. National bank's insurance subsidiary may acquire and hold a minority, noncontrolling interest in a title agency. The title agency can offer both lending and owner title insurance policies as agent, in connection with residential and commercial mortgage loans made by the bank, its affiliates, and by third parties and in cases where no loan is involved. The agency can also provide closing and escrow services and commercial and residential title abstracting services in connection with loans made by the bank, other lenders, and occasionally when no loan is involved. Conditional Approval No. 308 (April 8, 1999). [Editor's note: subsequent changes in the law have affected a national bank's authority to engage in title insurance activities. See 15 USC 6713.]

- **Insurance, Investment in Title Agency and Other Real Estate-Related Activities**. National bank's operating subsidiary may hold a minority investment in a company that engages in title insurance agency, real estate appraisal, loan closing, and other real estate loan-related and finder activities. Conditional Approval No. 332 (July 30, 1999).

- **Investment in Bank Holding Company as Consideration for Sale**. Where a group of financial institutions that jointly owned an EFT network was selling the network to a bank holding company, several national bank members of the group may acquire small equity interests in the bank holding company as consideration for their interests in the network. OCC Interpretive Letter No. 890 (May 15, 2000).

- **Investment in Fund for Solar-Energy Producing Facilities**. A national bank may invest in limited liability entities each of which will develop, acquire, install, and maintain solar energy-producing facilities and provide electricity for specified properties. Community Development Investment Letter No. 2008-1 (July 31, 2008).

- **Investments in Partnership With Native American Nations**. National bank's community development corporation (CDC) subsidiary may provide financial support and financial services to assist economic development efforts of Native American nations directed toward low- and moderate-income communities. Specific proposed activities of the CDC include: 1) providing financial literacy services; 2) buying, selling, and leasing real estate, for example, in partnership with local housing authorities; and 3) providing, servicing, and maintaining ATMs and ATM and debit cards. Approval of Bank's Self-Certification (December 20, 2002), National Bank Community Development Investments 2002 Directory.

- **Limited Interests in Private Investment Funds**. A national bank may acquire for limited periods of time, limited interests in private investment funds for which it serves as investment manager, as a way to structure its compensation. Because the bank's ownership of limited equity interests in the funds it advises is restricted to a context where the holding is integral to facilitating a recognized bank- permissible activity, such holdings are permissible as an incident to the bank- permissible investment management activities. OCC Interpretive Letter No. 940 (May 24, 2002).

- **Limited Partnership as an Operating Subsidiary**. A national bank may establish a limited partnership (LP) as an operating subsidiary, with a wholly owned limited liability company (LLC) as the limited partner and a wholly owned corporation as the general partner, to conduct a bank permissible activity. The LLC and corporation are each directly and wholly owned by the bank, resulting in the bank exercising, indirectly through the LLC and corporation, all economic and management control over the activities of the LP. The LP will hold participation interests in loans originated and purchased by the bank. Corporate Decision No. 2004-16 (September 10, 2004).

- **Limited-Purpose Bank**. A national bank may, pursuant to 12 USC 24(7) and the four-part test for noncontrolling equity investments by national banks, acquire and hold a noncontrolling equity interest in a limited-purpose, state-chartered bank that will limit its activities to those permissible for a banker's bank, i.e., the proposed bank will 1) take deposits from depository institutions; 2) buy and sell loan participations; 3) engage in lending transactions permissible for a banker's bank; and 4) provide correspondent services to depository institutions. OCC Interpretive Letter No. 970 (June 25, 2003).

- **Merchant Processing**. Application by a national bank to establish an operating subsidiary to engage in merchant processing activities through a limited partnership. The subsidiary will serve as the general partner and hold a 1-percent ownership interest in the limited partnership. A second affiliated national bank will be a limited partner and hold a 99-percent noncontrolling ownership interest in the limited partnership. The limited partnership will engage in proprietary merchant services in which applications are handled online through a software application that enables the sales force to review the application in real time. Corporate Decisions Nos. 582 and 583 (March 12, 2003).

- **Money Market Preferred Stock**. National banks may invest in money market preferred stock as Type III investment securities, provided the investment is marketable and not predominantly speculative in nature. OCC Interpretive Letter No. 781, reprinted in [1997 Transfer Binder] Fed. Banking L. Rep. (CCH) 81,208 (April 9, 1997). Municipal Revenue Bonds. Under 12 USC 24(Seventh), as amended by the Gramm-Leach-Bliley Act, a well-capitalized national bank may underwrite and deal in municipal revenue bonds issued by or on behalf of Puerto Rico. OCC Interpretive Letter No. 915 (August 15, 2001).

- **Mutual Fund Containing General Obligation and Municipal Revenue Bonds**. A national bank may invest in a mutual fund containing general obligation and municipal revenue bonds under 12 CFR 1.3(h)(2). The investment has a risk- weight dependent on the composition of the fund's assets, but in no event will the minimum risk-weight be less that 20 percent, and can be accounted for as either a "trading" or "available-for-sale" asset. OCC Interpretive Letter No. 912 (July 3, 2001).

- **Mutual Fund Shares**. National banks may purchase for their own accounts shares of any "investment company," with certain limitations. Shares of investment companies whose portfolios contain investments subject to the limits of 12 USC 24 may only be held in an account not in excess of either: 1) the amount equal to the appropriate investment limit for each security in the investment company or applied to the aggregate amount of the bank's pro rata holdings of that security in the investment company and the national bank's direct holding of that security; or 2) the most stringent investment limitation that would apply to any of the securities in the investment company's portfolio if those securities were purchased directly by the national bank. 12 CFR 1.4(e).

- **Noncontrolling Minority Interests (Including Limited Liability Companies)**. National banks may acquire noncontrolling minority investments in business entities if the entities: 1) engage in activities that are limited to those that are part of or incidental to the business of banking (or otherwise authorized for a national bank), 2) the national bank can prevent the company from engaging in activities that are not part of, or incidental to, the business of banking or be able to withdraw its investment, 3) the national bank's loss exposure is limited, as a legal and accounting matter, and the bank must not have open-ended liability for the obligation of the enterprise; and 4) the investment is convenient or useful to the bank in carrying out its business and is not a mere passive investment unrelated to that national bank's banking business. Conditional Approval No. 371 (March 20, 2000). The following are examples of these investments:

  – *Investment in LLC (Automobile Loans)*. National banks can acquire a noncontrolling investment, through an operating subsidiary, in a limited liability company (LLC) that provides automobile loans. Loan customers are people, who purchase cars over the Internet from other, non-national bank investors in the LLC. Conditional Approval No. 321 (July 28, 1999).

  – *Investments in LLCs (Cash Management, Electronic Payment, Information Reporting, and Data Processing Services)*. National bank's operating subsidiary can assume noncontrolling investments in limited liability companies that conduct cash management, electronic payment, information reporting, and data processing services. Conditional Approvals Nos. 324 (August 17, 1999) and 333 (October 19, 1999).

– *Investment in LLC (Credit Reporting Services).* National bank's operating subsidiary can hold a minority interest in a limited partnership to provide credit reporting services to the bank, its subsidiaries, affiliates, and eventually to nonaffiliated creditors. Conditional Approval No. 336 (November 2, 1999).

– *Investments in LLCs (Electronic Commerce).* National banks may acquire minority, noncontrolling interests in limited liability companies (LLC) that provide electronic commerce services and financial application software and related products. OCC Interpretive Letter No. 289 (May 15, 1989).

– *Investment in LLC (Employee Benefit Plans).* A national bank may acquire and hold noncontrolling equity interests in a limited liability company (LLC) that administers employee benefit plans for: 1) its investors, which are primarily financial institutions; and 2) other companies that have no equity interest in the LLC. OCC Interpretive Letter No. 994 (June 14, 2004).

– *Investment in LLC (Loans to and Investments in Medium- and Small-Sized Businesses.* National banks can acquire noncontrolling ownership interests in LLCs that make loans to and qualifying investments in medium- and small-sized businesses and invest in a small business investment company (SBIC), which, in turn, will make loans and invest in securities permissible under the SBIC Act. Conditional Approval No. 305 (March 15, 1999).

   o An SBIC is a privately organized and managed venture capital firm that is licensed and regulated by the Small Business Administration (SBA). An SBIC provides equity capital, long-term loans, debt-equity investments, and management assistance to qualifying small businesses, subject to significant regulatory restrictions. An SBIC is subject to limitations on the size and type of small businesses in which it may invest. Companies eligible for SBIC investments must have a net worth of under $18 million and under $6 million in net income at the time the investment is made. A national bank's aggregate SBIC investments are statutorily limited to 5 percent of the bank's capital and surplus.

   o Generally, an SBIC may invest in a variety of types of companies not limited to those that are financial in nature, but an SBIC may not invest in: other SBICS, finance and investment companies or leasing companies, unimproved real estate, companies with less than one-half of their assets and operations in the United States, passive or casual businesses (those not engaged in regular and continuous business operation), or companies that will use SBIC proceeds to invest in farmland.

o An SBIC may not have a controlling interest or own more than 50 percent of the voting equity of a company, in which it invests unless the SBIC has a plan of divestiture. In the latter case, the SBIC may have a controlling interest for up to seven years.

o An SBIC also must have experienced and qualified management, and to maintain diversification between an SBIC's investors and its management. In addition, an SBIC must conduct frequent investment valuations, file annual financial reports with the SBA, and submit to biennial compliance examinations by the SBA.

– *Investment in LLC (Origination of Residential Loans)*. National banks may make a direct, noncontrolling investment in a limited liability company (LLC) with an unaffiliated mortgage company as the other investor. The LLC may engage in the origination of residential mortgage loans with resale to investors in the secondary market. OCC Interpretive Letter No. 853, reprinted in [Current Transfer Binder] Fed. Banking L. Rep. (CCH) ¶ 81,310 (February 16, 1999).

– *Investment in LLC (Title Insurance)*. National banks can acquire a noncontrolling interest in an LLC that engages in title insurance agency activity, loan closing, and other activities in connection with consumer and commercial loans made by the bank or the bank's lending affiliate. OCC Interpretive Letter No. 842, reprinted in [1998-1999 Transfer Binder] Fed. Banking L. Rep. (CCH) ¶ 81,297 (September 28, 1998). [Editor's note: subsequent changes in the law have affected a national bank's authority to engage in title insurance activities. See 15 USC 6713.]

– *Second-Trust Deed Permanent Loan*. A national bank may invest, as a limited partner, in a community development entity formed under the federal new markets tax credit program which acquires real estate loan made to qualified, active, low-income community businesses. The specific investment fund invests in second-trust deed permanent loans on retail, office, commercial, and industrial projects. Approval of Bank's Self- Certification (November 22, 2004).

- **Nonprofit Making Loans to Low-Income Parents**. A national bank may invest in a private multi-service agency serving low-income parents transitioning from welfare to work. The agency provides small loans, for those workers who cannot get loans elsewhere, to help family members pay for unexpected expenses that can interfere with their ability to keep a job or stay in school. Community Development Investment Letter 2005-1 (April 7, 2005).

- **Other Issuers**. If an issuer does not fall within specified criteria for other categories of investment securities, a national bank may treat a debt security as an investment security for purposes of Part 1, if the national bank concludes, on the basis of estimates that the bank reasonably believes reliable, that the obligor will be able to satisfy its obligations under that security, and the national bank believes that the security may be sold with reasonable promptness at a price that corresponds reasonably to its fair value. The aggregate par value of these securities may not exceed 5 percent of the national bank's capital and surplus. 12 CFR 1.4(i), OCC Interpretive Letter No. 779, reprinted in [1997 Transfer Binder] Fed. Banking L. Rep. (CCH) ¶ 81,206 (April 3, 1997).

- **Performance Note Loans (PNL).** National banks may purchase PNLs, issued by affiliates of private mortgage insurers, as loans. A PNL is a debt security bearing a variable interest rate linked to the performance of the mortgage loans that the lender originated and the mortgage insurer insured. OCC Interpretive Letter No. 833, reprinted in [1998-1999 Transfer Binder] Fed. Banking L. Rep. (CCH) ¶ 81,287 (July 8, 1998), 834, reprinted in [1998-1999 Transfer Binder] Fed. Banking L. Rep. (CCH) ¶ 81,288 (July 8, 1998).

- **Private Investment Fund.** National banks may acquire for their own account beneficial interests in a privately offered investment fund that would invest in loans, cash and cash equivalents, and an offshore fund that invests solely in loans. National banks may hold interests in the fund either as securities under the reliable estimates standard of Part 1 or as loan participations. OCC Interpretive Letter No. 911 (June 4, 2001).

- **Public Welfare Investments.** National banks have express authority to invest, directly or indirectly (such as through community development corporations), in investments designed primarily to promote the public welfare. These investments are limited to 5 percent of the national bank's unimpaired capital stock (actually paid in) and surplus fund. However, the OCC may approve investments up to a total of 10 percent of unimpaired capital and surplus for national banks that are at least adequately capitalized, if the OCC determines that an investment over the 5- percent limit will pose no significant risk to the deposit insurance fund. In no case may a public welfare investment expose a national bank to unlimited liability. 12 USC 24(Eleventh).

  - *Public Welfare Activities.* The types of activities that are considered to be public welfare investments include, but may not be limited to, those that provide or support affordable housing, community services, or permanent jobs for low- or moderate-income individuals; equity or debt financing for small businesses; and area revitalization or stabilization. 12 CFR 24.3(a). For example, national banks may invest in limited partnerships investing in affordable housing projects approved for low-income housing tax credits. E.g., letter from Janice A. Booker, Director, Community Development Division, to Yasumasa Gomi, Chairman of the Board, President, and CEO, The Bank of California (December 22, 1992). A national bank also may make an equity investment in a real estate investment trust that focuses primarily on community development activities, such as making investments in and purchasing loans that will benefit low- and moderate-income individuals and areas. Letter from Janice A. Booker, Director, Community Development Division, to Michael E. Bleier, General Counsel, Mellon Bank (February 25, 1999). National banks may also invest in and form community partnerships with community development financial institutions. Letter from Janice A. Booker, Director, Community Development Division, to Larry Hawkins, President, Unity National Bank (November 16, 1998).

– *Public Welfare Purpose*. By regulation, public welfare investments must primarily benefit low- and moderate-income individuals, low- and moderate-income areas, or other areas targeted for redevelopment by local, state, tribal or federal government (including federal enterprise communities and federal empowerment zones). 12 CFR 24.3(a). A majority of the activities of an investment must benefit the targeted beneficiaries in order for the activity to be designed primarily to promote the public welfare, but the remainder of the activities need not. OCC Interpretive Letter No. 837, reprinted in [1998-1999 Transfer Binder] Fed. Banking L. Rep. (CCH) ¶ 81,291 (September 4, 1998).

- **Purchase of Bonds and Other Tax Exempt Instruments Issued by Government Agencies**. A national bank may purchase preferred shares in a trust that acquires and owns tax-exempt participating and nonparticipating first mortgage bonds and other tax-exempt instruments that are issued by various state or local government, agencies or authorities. The proceeds from the bonds are used for financing affordable housing development and rehabilitation, and most of those properties also benefit from the use of federal low-income housing tax credits. Community Development Investment Letter 2003-3 (September 30, 2003).

- **Purchase of Shares in CDC Subsidiary of Affiliated National Bank**. Four affiliated national banks may each purchase shares in an existing community development corporation (CDC) subsidiary that previously had been formed and capitalized by a fifth affiliated national bank. As a result of the new investments, the CDC subsidiary expanded its products and services to the states that the new shareholders served. Approval of Banks' Self-Certifications (January 30, 2002; January 31, 2002; May 9, 2002; and May 9, 2002), National Bank Community Development Investments 2002 Directory.

- **Real Estate (Non-Thrift/Bank Premises)**. Aside from property necessary for the transaction of its business, the authority of national banks to purchase and lease real estate has been limited to special circumstances, including purchasing and leasing real estate for municipal purposes (including purchasing vacant land for this purpose) and purchasing residences of bank employees who have been transferred. In addition, national banks may purchase, hold, and convey real estate as mortgaged to them or conveyed as security for or in satisfaction of debts previously contracted, and as purchased at sales under judgments, decrees, or mortgages held by a bank or to secure debts due to it. National bank may not hold real estate conveyed to it to satisfy debts previously contracted for longer than five years, unless a period of up to an additional five years is approved by the OCC 12 USC 29; 12 CFR 7.1000; 12 CFR 34; OCC Interpretive Letter No. 847, reprinted in [1998-1999 Transfer Binder] Fed. Banking L. Rep. (CCH) ¶ 81,302 (October 28, 1998).

- **Reinsurance Company**. Insurance agency operating subsidiary of a national bank may make a minority equity investment in a Bermuda reinsurance company that is necessary for the subsidiary to obtain liability insurance for itself. OCC Interpretive Letter No. 965 (February 24, 2003).

- **Reinsurer, Holding Noncontrolling Interests**. National banks may hold a noncontrolling interest in an insurance company that reinsures mortgage life, mortgage accidental death, and mortgage disability insurance on loans originated by the lenders with an ownership interest in the insurance company. OCC Interpretive Letter No. 835 reprinted in [1998-99 Transfer Binder] Fed. Banking L. Rep. (CCH) 81-289 (July 31, 1998).

- **Residential Mortgage-Related Securities**. National banks may invest in certain investment grade residential mortgage-related securities. 12 CFR 1.3(e).

- **Retention of Stock Holdings Resulting From Conversion**. Bank may retain shares of stock that it received as a result of being a policyholder of a mutual life insurance company that converted to stock form. The stock is not an impermissible purchase of stock, but a byproduct of the permissible activity of purchasing life insurance for the bank's needs. Divestiture of the stock will be required only if safety and soundness concerns arise in the future. This is an issue that many banks will face, as increasing numbers of life insurance companies "demutualize." OCC Interpretive Letter No. 905 (January 29, 2001).

- **Second-Trust Deed Permanent Loan**. A national bank may invest, as a limited partner, in a community development entity formed under the federal new markets tax credit program which acquires real estate loan made to qualified, active, low-income community businesses. The specific investment fund invests in second-trust deed permanent loans on retail, office, commercial, and industrial projects. Approval of Bank's Self-Certification (November 22, 2004).

- **Small Business Investments**. National banks may invest in investment-grade, small business-related securities that are fully secured by interests in a pool of loans to numerous obligors. National bank investments in securities of any one issuer rated investment grade in the third or fourth highest categories may not exceed 25 percent of the national bank's capital and surplus. In addition, national banks may invest in small business investment companies (SBIC) in an aggregate amount of up to 5 percent of the national bank's capital and surplus. 12 USC 24(Seventh); 12 CFR 1.3(a); OCC Interpretive Letter No. 373, reprinted in [1985-1987 Transfer Binder] Fed. Banking L. Rep. (CCH) ¶ 85,543 (November 13, 1986).

- **Stock Warrants**. A national bank that permissibly acquired stock warrants of borrower (12 CFR 7.1006) may, under the specific circumstances and conditions represented by the bank, exercise the warrants in order to immediately sell the resulting stock. OCC Interpretive Letter No. 992 (May 10, 2004).

- **Streamlined Approval for CDC Investments in Connection With Thrift Conversion Into National Bank**. Federal thrift may retain its existing CDC investments provided that they qualify as public welfare investments under 12 CFR 24 without a separate filing under 12 CFR 24. The OCC will review the CDC investments in connection with the conversion application and will determine whether the investment is approved in connection with the conversion decision. Corporate Decision 2002-7 (June 16, 2001).

- **Stock in Life Insurance Underwriter**. National bank may accept and retain stock in a life insurance underwriter that it received as a result of being a policyholder of the company, which was converting from mutual to stock form ("demutualization"). OCC Interpretive Letter No. 901 (June 29, 2000).

- **Structured Finance Transaction**. A national bank may acquire an interest in an operating subsidiary in which a financial services company chartered and operating in the United Kingdom also will have an interest. The operating subsidiary was created for the purpose of facilitating a complex structured finance transaction by which the national bank will lend money to the financial services company. Corporate Decision Letter No. 646 (June 28, 2004).

- **Tax Credits**. A national bank may make a noncontrolling investment in a limited liability company (LLC) in order to generate new markets tax credits. The LLC may engage in activities not permissible for national banks as long as the bank's investment in a series of membership units is segregated from all other investments and used only for bank permissible purposes. OCC Interpretive Letter No. 996 (July 6, 2004).

- **Transitional Housing**. A national bank may invest, through its subsidiary community development corporation (CDC), in the acquisition and rehabilitation of a single-family dwelling to provide transitional housing for the homeless. The CDC will own and manage the property and residents of the facility will receive case management support from an established nonprofit social services provider. After successful completion of the transitional housing program, for a term of one to two years, qualified residents would be provided an option to purchase the dwelling. Approval of Bank's Self-Certification (April 26, 2004).

- **Trust Bank Stock**. National banks may establish operating subsidiaries to serve as a general partner in a partnership that will own a trust company. National banks may acquire a minority interest in a limited purpose trust bank. OCC Interpretive Letter Nos. 697, reprinted in [1995-1996 Transfer Binder] Fed. Banking L. Rep. (CCH) ¶ 81,012 (November 15, 1995), 831, reprinted in [1997-1998 Transfer Binder] Fed. Banking L. Rep. (CCH) ¶ 81,285 (June 8, 1998).

- **Trust Preferred Securities Purchased as Investment Securities**. National banks may invest in trust preferred securities that meet applicable rating and marketability requirements as Type III investment securities under 12 CFR 1. OCC Interpretive Letter No. 777, reprinted in [1997 Transfer Binder] Fed. Banking L. Rep. (CCH) ¶ 81,204 (April 8, 1997).

- **Trust Preferred Securities Purchased Under Lending Authority**. A national bank may purchase under its lending authority, trust preferred securities that are not marketable and thus do not qualify as investment securities under Part I, subject to the lending limits of 12 USC 84 and the requirements of Banking Circular 181 (REV). OCC Interpretive Letter No. 908 (April 23, 2001).

- **U.S. Government-Sponsored Corporation Securities**. National banks may invest, without limitation, in obligations of Fannie Mae, Ginnie Mae, Freddie Mac, Sallie Mae, FHLBanks, Federal Finance Bank, and Farmer Mac 12 USC 24(Seventh). National banks may purchase preferred stock of Freddie Mac and Sallie Mae. OCC Interpretive Letter (December 3, 1992); OCC Interpretive Letter No. 577, reprinted in [1991-1992 Transfer Binder] Fed. Banking L. Rep. (CCH) ¶ 83,347 (April 6, 1992). National banks may invest in the stock of FHLB, in excess of minimum membership requirements. OCC Interpretive Letter No. 755, reprinted in [1996-1997 Transfer Binder] Fed. Banking L. Rep. (CCH) ¶ 81,119 (October 3, 1996). National banks may purchase stock of Fanner Mac, OCC Interpretive Letter No. 427 reprinted in [1988-1989 Transfer Binder] Fed. Banking L. Rep. (CCH) ¶ 85,651 (May 7, 1988), and Fannie Mae, 12 USC 1718(f). In addition, national banks may invest in obligations of the TVA, Postal Service, and various international development banks, provided investments in any one of these latter entities do not exceed 10 percent of capital and surplus. 12 USC 24(Seventh); 12 CFR 1.20. National bank may hold up to 5 percent of its capital and surplus in stock of state housing corporations. 12 USC 24(Seventh).

- **U.S., State, and Local Government Securities**. National banks may invest in securities issued or guaranteed by the United States or any agency of the United States, as well as general obligations of any state or political subdivision thereof and the Washington Metropolitan Area Transit Authority. 12 USC 24(Seventh); 12 CFR Part 1.

- **Use of New Markets Tax Credits**. National bank may invest in wholly owned subsidiary that, in turn, makes an investment in a fund that is certified by the U.S. Department of the Treasury as a "community development entity." The fund will provide debt and equity financing for retail, office, commercial, distribution, industrial mixed-use, and community facility projects in targeted low- and moderate-income areas. The fund is anticipated to earn federal new markets tax credits that will be usable by the bank and other investors. Approval of Bank's Self-Certification (August 28, 2002), National Bank Community Development Investments 2002 Directory.

- **Various Activities of CDC Subsidiary**. A national bank's community development corporation (CDC) subsidiary may conduct various community and economic development activities that primarily benefit low- and moderate-income individuals, low- and moderate-income areas, or other areas targeted for redevelopment by local, state, federal, or tribal governments. The approved activities of the CDC include: 1) providing financing to a corporation that owns and operates a charter school, funded by the state, that educates "at-risk" students, who are primarily low- and moderate-income and have exhibited behavioral or drug problems in other schools; 2) providing financing at reduced rates to low- and moderate-income families that received subsidies under state and federal government programs for the purchase of their first homes; 3) investing in an entity that renovated a commercial building leased to a state government agency that provides training to unemployed low- and moderate-income individuals and assists them in finding employment; 4) financing the education of a medical student who had committed to work after graduation for a facility that provides medical services to low-income families; 5) providing working capital for a convenience and hardware store in a low- and moderate-income community; and 6) investing in a fund that provides financing for developing and operating affordable housing and is anticipated to earn federal low-income housing tax credits that will be usable by the bank. Approval of Bank's Prior Approval Requests and Self-Certifications (April 16, 2002; May 3, 2002; May 3, 2002; July 18, 2002; September 23, 2002; and September 23, 2002), National Bank Community Development Investments 2002 Directory.

- **Warrants for Common Stock**. National banks may establish operating subsidiaries to acquire warrants for common stock. Conditional Approval No. 319 (July 26, 1999).

Community Development

- **Fund Comprising SBA Guaranteed Loans**. A national bank may make an investment in a fund which invests in the federally guaranteed portion of Small Business Administration 7(a) loans. Publication pending (February 8, 2006).

- **Fund for Construction of Agricultural Facilities**. A national bank may make an investment in a community and economic development entity that funds construction of agricultural-product receiving bins, which will increase the tax base and produce jobs in a low- and moderate-income area. Community Development Investment Letter 2009-2 (January 6, 2009).

- **Fund for Construction of Rent-to-Own Affordable Rental Housing**. A national bank may make an investment in a community and economic development entity which will use new markets tax credits, for the construction of a rent-to-own affordable housing complex in a low- and moderate-income area. Community Development Investment Letter 2009-5 (June 17, 2009).

- **Fund to Construct an Industrial Facility on Indian Reservation**. A national bank may make an investment in a community and economic development entity that constructs an industrial facility that will produce jobs on an Indian reservation in a low- and moderate-income area. Community Development Investment Letter 2009-3 (March 9, 2009).

- **Fund to Renovate and Lease a Residential Drug and Alcohol Treatment Center**. A national bank may make an investment in a community and economic development entity, which uses new markets tax credits, for the renovation and lease of a residential drug and alcohol treatment center in a low- and moderate income area. Community Development Investment Letter 2009-4 (June 17 2009).

- **Fund to Provide Low-Cost Products and Services**. A national bank may make an investment in community and economic development entities that have a dedicated adherence to provide low-cost financial products and services for underbanked and low-to-moderate income consumers. Community Development Investment Letter [No. pending] (April 5, 2011).

- **Investment in Fund to Install Photovoltaic System in Low-Income Housing Tax Credit Project**. A national bank may make an investment in a Community and Economic Development Entity that will install photovoltaic systems in low income housing tax credit projects. These systems will qualify for renewable energy tax credits. Community Development Investment Letter No. 2009-6 (December 16, 2009).

- **Investment in Fund for Solar–Energy-Producing Facilities**. A national bank may make an equity investment to acquire a membership interest in a fund (the company) established as a limited liability company that will sign a master lease for a solar-energy project financed by the company. The managing member of the company is a renewable-energy utility company that designed, insured, and maintained customized solar systems for industrial, commercial, and municipal enterprises. The investment primarily benefits low- and moderate-income areas Community Development Precedent Letter 2009-01 (February 17, 2009).

- **Investment in the Construction and Sale of Single Family Properties**. A national bank's subsidiary community development corporation may invest in the construction of single family homes, which are then resold, located in low- or moderate-income communities. Community Development Investment Letter 2007-2 (October 11, 2007).

- **Investment in the Renovation and Resale of Single Family Properties**. A national bank's subsidiary community development corporation may invest in the acquisition and renovation of single family homes, which are then resold, located in low- or moderate-income communities. Community Development Investment Letter 2007-1 (August 17, 2007).

- **Stabilizing Communities**. National banks may use a variety of funding and financing tools, such as the Department of Housing and Urban Development's Neighborhood Stabilization Program and the new markets and low-income housing tax credit programs to facilitate the sale of foreclosed properties. Stabilization activities may qualify for consideration under the Community Reinvestment Act. "Property Disposition: Exploring Different Approaches for Preserving Affordable Housing Opportunities," Community Developments Insights (March 2009).

Other Investments

- **Additional Expenditures on Other Real Estate Owned (OREO) Property**. National banks, under some conditions, may make additional expenditures on OREO property in order to facilitate the disposal of the OREO. Banks cannot make additional expenditures on OREO property for speculative purposes, such as ground-up construction and sale of completed residences in order to achieve greater return. 12 CFR 34.86(a). OCC Interpretive Letter 1129 (February 3, 2011).

- **Bank Premises.** Additional explanation of rationale for prior Interpretive Letters stating permissibility of a national bank to hold a building containing retail and office space and commercial facilities for lodging out-of-town bank visitors. OCC Interpretive Letter No. 1053 (January 31, 2006).

- **Bank Premises—Long Term Ground Lease.** Letter concludes that it would be permissible under 12 USC 29 for a bank to enter into a long-term ground lease with an unrelated third party of property that it has owned and used as bank premises for three decades. OCC Interpretive Letter No. 1072 (September 15, 2006).

- **Equity Investment Financing for Wind Energy Project.** Additional explanation of rationale for prior Interpretive Letter stating a national bank may provide financing for a wind energy project by making an equity investment in the project, because the transaction is structured to be the functional equivalent of a secured financing. Structuring the transaction in this manner permits the bank to capture tax benefits enacted to promote the flow of capital to renewable sources of energy. OCC Interpretive Letter No. 1048a (February 27, 2006) and OCC Interpretive Letter No. 1053 (January 31, 2006).

- **Exchange of DPC Real Estate for Equity Interest.** An OCC Interpretive Letter disapproved a proposal for national banks to exchange DPC real estate for an equity interest in an entity which would aggregate OREO from multiple financial institutions, and addressed legal, supervisory, and accounting issues. OCC Interpretive Letter No. 1128 (October 1, 2010).

- **Investments in Complex Structure With Indirect Credit Default Swap Index Exposure.** A national trust company may sponsor a closed-end investment fund that will be exempt from registration under the Investment Company Act of 1940. The fund invests in preferred shares issued by companies engaged in credit default swap activities involving embedded credit leverage. National banks of a specified asset size with requisite sophistication may purchase the fund shares pursuant to 12 CFR 1.3(h)(2),subject to safety and soundness standards. OCC Interpretive Letter No. 1047 (December 20, 2005).

- **Noncontrolling Investment in Fraud Prevention Company.** A national bank can hold a noncontrolling investment in a company that offers fraud prevention, identity verification, credential validation, and payment/deposit risk services to financial institutions and other companies in the financial industry. OCC Interpretive Letter No. 1077 (January 11, 2007).

- **Retention of MasterCard Stock.** A national bank may retain stock received in IPO of MasterCard, Inc., because it is a byproduct of permissible membership in MasterCard. OCC Interpretive Letter No. 1075 (November 14, 2006).

PREEMPTION

- **In General**. Federal preemption of state law restrictions applies to activities of national banks whether conducted at branches or nonbranch facilities (loan production offices (LPO), deposit production offices (DPO), automated teller machines (ATM), remote service units (RSU)) or through operations over the Internet.

  - *Affiliation*. States generally may not prevent or restrict national banks or their affiliates from affiliating with any entity, including a securities or insurance firm, as authorized by the Gramm-Leach-Bliley Act (GLBA) or any other federal law. 15 USC 6701 (as added by section 104 of GLBA).

  - *American Bankers Association v. Brown*. The Supreme Court denied certiorari in a Ninth Circuit Court of Appeals case. The American Bankers Association sought review of the Ninth Circuit's decision reversing the federal district court. The district court had concluded that express preemption provisions of the Fair Credit Reporting Act preempted the California Financial Information Privacy Act in its entirety, allowing affiliates to share any information without regard to information-sharing limitations imposed by state law. The Ninth Circuit interpreted the term "information" to mean only information that met the definition of "consumer report" in the Fair Credit Reporting Act. American Bankers Association v. Lockyer, 541 F.3d 1214 (9th Cir. 2008), cert. denied, 129 S.Ct. 2893 (June 29, 2009).

  - *Annual Reports, Fees for Extension of Consumer Credit: Idaho*. Provisions of Idaho Consumer Credit Code requiring annual reports and payment of fees as a condition to being permitted to extend consumer credit are preempted by federal law. OCC Interpretive Letter (May 6, 1993).

  - *Annuities: Connecticut*. A Connecticut statute that requires all sellers of variable annuities to be licensed by the state is preempted. OCC Interpretive Letter No. 623, reprinted in [1993-1994 Transfer Binder] Fed. Banking L. Rep. (CCH) ¶ 83,512 (May 10, 1993).

  - *Annuities: Florida*. The anti-affiliation provisions of the Florida Insurance Code, and provisions requiring national banks to give notice and obtain authorization to engage in the sale of annuities, as well as implementing regulations, conflict with the authority of national banks to sell annuities as agent and are therefore preempted. OCC Interpretive Letter (July 13, 1993).

  - *Annuities: Texas*. Texas insurance licensing laws that prevent or significantly interfere with a national bank's authority to sell annuities as agent are preempted, but other state laws are not preempted; applicable federal securities laws apply to the sale of these products. OCC Interpretive Letter No. 749, reprinted in [1996-1997 Transfer Binder] Fed. Banking L. Rep. (CCH) ¶ 81,114 (September 13, 1996).

- *Applicability of Doctrine of Complete Preemption to Usury Suits Brought in State Court.* Reversing the 11th Circuit, the Supreme Court, in a 7–2 decision, held that a usury case brought against a national bank in state court could be removed to federal court under the doctrine of complete preemption. Complete preemption is a corollary to the well-pleaded complaint rule that a claim that falls within an exclusively federal cause of action necessarily presents a federal question warranting removal. Beneficial National Bank v. Anderson, 537 U.S. 1169 (2003).

- *Applicability of State Laws That Restrict Information Sharing With Affiliates.* A U.S. District Court held that provisions of the Fair Credit Reporting Act preempt local ordinances that impose restrictions on the sharing of confidential consumer information between financial institutions and their affiliates. As to the sharing of information with affiliates, the court decided that it need not address whether an express provision of the Gramm-Leach-Bliley Act (GLBA) also preempted the ordinances. However, as for the sharing of confidential consumer information with third parties, the court found that neither GLBA nor the National Bank Act preempts the ordinances. The OCC filed an amicus brief jointly with groups of bank amici and insurer amici. Upon appeal before the U.S. Court of Appeals for the Ninth Circuit, the defendant municipalities notified the Ninth Circuit that they had repealed the ordinances in dispute in the litigation and asked the court to dismiss the banks' appeal as moot and vacate the district court's decision in its entirety. The banks responded, agreeing that the appeal was moot, but that only that portion of the district court decision on appeal, the decision that section 104 of the GLBA did not preempt the municipal ordinances, should be vacated. Bank of America v. Daly City, 279 F.Supp. 2d 1118 (N.D. Cal. 2003).

- *Applicability of State Laws to National Bank Operating Subsidiaries.* The OCC has issued a number of letters addressing the applicability of state laws with respect to activities conducted in national bank operating subsidiaries. These letters confirm that a particular subsidiary of a national bank is subject to the OCC's examination and supervision pursuant to 12 CFR 5.34(e)(3); explain that, under 12 CFR 7.4006, state laws apply to national bank operating subsidiaries to the same extent that those laws apply to the national bank itself; and conclude that state restrictions or conditions, including licensing requirements, do not apply to the national bank operating subsidiary. Letters were issued to appropriate state regulatory authorities (or to the bank or its counsel) with respect to laws in eight states and one city including: Pennsylvania, Michigan, New Hampshire, Connecticut, Rhode Island, Iowa, Louisiana, Maine, and the city of Las Vegas, Nevada.

- *Application of New Jersey Consumer Fraud Act.* Letter filed with the court responding to the parties' request on whether federal law authorizing national banks to make real estate loans preempted application of the New Jersey Consumer Fraud Act to loans that were originated by a third party and were held by the national banks as trustees for two issues of mortgage-backed securities. The OCC concluded that the banks were not engaged in real estate lending as a result of the transactions involved and, therefore, the OCC's real estate lending regulations did not preempt the state law. OCC Interpretive Letter No. 1016 (January 14, 2005) submitted in Wells Fargo Bank, Minnesota, N.A. v. Harris, No. ESX-L-4676-02; and Bank One v. Feinstein, No. F-11450-00 (N.J. Superior Court: Chancery Division, Essex County).

– *ATM Fees.* Local laws in California purporting to bar national banks from "surcharging" automated teller machine (ATM) users who are not bank account holders are preempted by the National Bank Act, which authorizes national banks to provide ATM services and to charge for the services they provide. Bank of America, N.A., et al. v. City and County of San Francisco, CA, et al., 215 F 3d 1132 (9th Cir., March 31, 2000), aff'g CC-99-4817-VRW (N.D. Ca. November 11, 1999).

– *ATM Fees.* Two national banks and a savings and loan association brought suit challenging municipal ordinances prohibiting banks from charging ATM fees to non-depositors. After obtaining preliminary injunctive relief from the regulations, the banks obtained permanent injunctive relief from the district court. A panel of the U.S. Court of Appeals for the Ninth Circuit affirmed, holding that, as for national banks, the National Bank Act and the OCC's regulations preempted the ordinances. A rehearing petition filed by the City and County of San Francisco was denied. OCC filed an amicus brief with the Ninth Circuit. Bank of America, et al. v. City and County of San Francisco, 309 F. 3d 551 (9th Cir. 2002).

– *ATM Operations.* State laws in Massachusetts that purport to restrict the ability of a national bank located elsewhere to establish and operate automated teller machines in those states are preempted. The Massachusetts law imposes a reciprocity requirement; Florida requires banks to be authorized to do business in Florida, which the Florida Banking Department interprets to mean, in the context of an out-of-state bank, a bank that has established a branch in Florida pursuant to Florida's branching laws. OCC Interpretive Letter No. 939 (October 15, 2001).

– *ATM Restrictions*: Colorado. Portions of the Colorado Electronic Funds Transfer Act prohibiting national banks from placing their names on ATMs and giving the state regulatory authority over national bank ATMs are preempted. OCC Interpretive Letter No. 789, reprinted in [1997 Transfer Binder] Fed. Banking L. Rep. (CCH) ¶ 81,216 (June 27, 1997).

– *Auction of Certificates of Deposit Over the Internet.* Pennsylvania laws that purport to regulate the auction of certificates of deposit over the Internet, by requiring auctioneers to be licensed by the Pennsylvania Board of Auctioneer Examiners, pay a licensing fee, and keep records of sales of property at auction, are preempted because they conflict with federal law authorizing national banks to conduct the permissible activities of deposit-taking and marketing and OCC regulations authorizing national banks to use the Internet to do so. The state laws at issue also would violate the OCC's exclusive visitorial powers over national banks. Preemption determination (March 7, 2000). *Federal Register*, 65 FR 15037 (March 20, 2000).

- *Checking Accounts: New Jersey.* The New Jersey Consumer Checking Act is preempted. OCC Interpretive Letter No. 572, reprinted in [1991-1992 Transfer Binder] Fed. Banking L. Rep. (CCH) ¶ 83,342 (January 15, 1992).

- *City of Cleveland v. Ameriquest Mortgage Services, Inc.* The district court issued a decision on May 15, 2009, granting the defendants' motion to dismiss the city's state law nuisance claim against mortgage securitizers, including several national banks. Although the OCC filed an amicus brief supporting national banks' argument that the state law nuisance action was preempted by federal law, the court dismissed the city's complaint on state law grounds. The city has filed an appeal that is pending before the Sixth Circuit Court of Appeals. City of Cleveland v. Ameriquest Mortgage Services, Inc., 621 F.Supp.2d (N.D. Ohio 2009), appeal docketed, No.09-3608 (6th Cir. May 27, 2009).

- *Clarifications of the OCC's Determination and Order Preempting the Georgia Fair Lending Act (GFLA).* Two OCC letters clarify aspects of the OCC determination and order concluding that the GFLA was preempted with respect to national banks and their operating subsidiaries. The determination and order was published in the *Federal Register* at 68 FR 46264 (August 5, 2003). One letter describes the provisions of the GFLA Act that are not preempted by the determination and order; explains that questions about the applicability of any state insurance sales laws to national banks are outside the scope of the determination and order and the OCC's new preemption rule; and discusses the applicability of the determination and order and the preemption rule to mortgage brokers. OCC Interpretive Letter No. 1000 (April 2, 2004). A second letter further clarifies the applicability to mortgage brokers of the determination and order the OCC's final preemption rule. OCC Interpretive Letter No. 1002 (May 13, 2004).

- *Consumer Credit, Examination Fees: Idaho.* Provisions of the Idaho Consumer Credit Code that impose licensing requirements as a condition to extending consumer credit, recordkeeping and reporting requirements, and assessments of fees to defray the costs of supervision and examination are preempted. OCC Interpretive Letter (February 9, 1995).

- *Consumer Protection.* The OCC addresses concerns about the impact of the OCC's preemption and visitorial powers rules on consumers, explaining the agency's approach to preventing predatory lending practices, and describing its record of taking appropriate action to protect consumers if the agency finds such practices have occurred. OCC Interpretive Letter No. 999 (March 9, 2004).

- *Contacts From State Officials.* Applicability of state laws to national banks and their operating subsidiaries – and the authority to enforce those laws – raises complex issues of both federal preemption and the statutory authority of the OCC as the supervisor and regulator of national banks. Because of the complexity of these issues, national banks should consult with the OCC if they are contacted by state officials seeking information that may constitute an attempt to exercise visitorial or enforcement powers over the bank. State officials are also encouraged to contact the OCC if they have information indicating that a national bank may be violating federal or applicable state law or if they seek information from a national bank. OCC Advisory Letter 2002-9 (November 25, 2002).

– *Credit Card Operations, Licensing, Visitation, and Fees: Iowa.* Provisions of the Iowa Lender Credit Card Act regarding state licensing, supervision, and permissible rates and fees for credit card lenders are preempted for national banks. OCC Interpretive Letter (February 4, 1992).

– *Credit Cards Finance Charges: Massachusetts.* A Massachusetts law that requires the reporting of credit card finance charges and fees to the state is preempted. OCC Interpretive Letter No. 616, reprinted in [1992-1993 Transfer Binder] Fed. Banking L. Rep. (CCH) ¶ 83,456 (February 26, 1993).

– *Cuomo v. Clearinghouse Association.* On June 29, the U.S. Supreme Court delivered its decision in the case of Cuomo v. Clearing House Association. The case involved an attempt by the New York State Attorney General to obtain non-public information from national banks in connection with an investigation over alleged fair lending violations. The banks and the OCC argued that the state's demand was an illegal encroachment on the OCC's exclusive "visitorial" powers to inspect, examine, supervise, and regulate. The Supreme Court agreed with the OCC that the New York Attorney General could not proceed as he had attempted to do, but clarified the scope of the OCC's exclusive visitorial powers and concluded that those powers would not block a state law-enforcement official from bringing an action in court against a national bank to enforce a non-preempted state law. Cuomo v. Clearinghouse Association, 557 U.S. (2009).

– *Debt Cancellation Contracts: Texas.* A Texas administrative interpretation that the Texas Credit Code prohibits national banks from offering debt cancellation contracts is preempted. OCC Interpretive Letter (November 2, 1992).

– *Debt Cancellation Contracts and Debt Suspension Agreements (12 CFR 37).* The OCC published a final rule that addresses debt cancellation contracts and debt suspension agreements. The purposes of the customer protections are to facilitate customers' informed choice about whether to purchase debt cancellation contracts and debt suspension agreements, based on an understanding of the costs, benefits, and limitations of the products and to discourage inappropriate or abusive sales practices. The final rule also promotes safety and soundness by requiring national banks that provide these products to maintain adequate loss reserves. The final rule was published in the *Federal Register* at 67 FR 58962 (September 19, 2002). The OCC subsequently delayed, pending further action, the date for mandatory compliance with certain provisions of the rule for national banks offering debt cancellation or debt suspension products through a non-exclusive agent in connection with closed-end consumer credit. See *Federal Register*, 68 FR 35283 (June 13, 2003).

- *Determination and Order Preempting the Georgia Fair Lending Act (GFLA).* The OCC issued a determination and order in response to a request from National City Bank, National City Bank of Indiana, and their operating subsidiaries, National City Mortgage Company and First Franklin Financial Company. The request asked the OCC to determine whether the GFLA applied to the banks and their operating subsidiaries, and to issue an appropriate order. The OCC concluded that the provisions of the GFLA affecting national banks' real estate lending are preempted by federal law and, accordingly, that the GFLA does not apply to National City or to any other national bank or national bank operating subsidiary that engages in real estate lending activities in Georgia. The determination and order was published in the *Federal Register* at 68 FR 46264 (August 5, 2003).

- *Document Preparation Fee.* State court ruled that Indiana law regulating the practice of law prohibits national bank from charging a document preparation fee in connection with its mortgage lending program. The Indiana Court of Appeals affirmed that only licensed attorneys may charge a fee for filling out mortgages and notes used in making real estate loans and rejected the Bank's argument that the state law was preempted by OCC regulations authorizing national banks to charge fees in connection with their authorized banking activities. Charter One Mortgage Corp. v. Condra, 847 N.E.2d 207 (Ind. App. May 12, 2006), oral argument held December 7, 2006 and petition to transfer granted the same date.

- *Document Preparation Fees.* A state court in Michigan held that a national bank had a right to charge document preparation fees in connection with its mortgage lending activities without being subject to the restrictions on such fees imposed by Michigan law. Brannam v. The Huntington Mortgage Co., Case No. 00-40439-CH (Cir. Ct., Muskegon City, MI, February 2, 2004).

- *Document Preparation Fees.* Court in Illinois upheld the dismissal of 37 cases, consolidated for appeal, in which the plaintiffs sought to recover restitution or damages for document preparation fees that they had paid in connection with obtaining real estate mortgages. The OCC had filed an amicus brief with the court below in support of a national bank's position that federal law authorizes the bank to charge document preparation fees. Although the appellate court dismissed the cases on a different ground, this did not vacate the decision of the trial court. Jenkins v. Concorde Acceptance, Consol. Appeal No. 02-2738 (App. Ct., Ill., December 31, 2003).

- *Document Preparation Fees.* In a unanimous opinion, the Illinois Supreme Court affirmed two decisions of the Illinois Court of Appeals that dismissed complaints in 38 lawsuits, consolidated for appeal, where the plaintiffs alleged that various lenders, including a national bank operating subsidiary, engaged in the unauthorized practice of law by charging a fee for preparing real estate mortgage loan documents. The court concluded that a company engages in the practice of law by preparing loan documents, such as the note and the mortgage. Under Illinois law, however, a party to a transaction is permitted to prepare the documents memorializing that transaction.

Thus, the court held that state law permits lenders, including national bank subsidiaries, to charge fees for preparing loan documents. King. v. First Capital Financial Service Corp., 828 N.E.2d 1155 (2005).

- *Document Preparation Fees.* OCC filed an amicus brief on July 26, 2005, in the Indiana Court of Appeals supporting the bank and its operating subsidiary in their appeal of the trial court's denial of the bank's motion to dismiss a class action lawsuit seeking a refund of document preparation fees collected from real estate mortgage customers. The OCC brief explains that the National Bank Act and 12 CFR 7.4002 authorize the bank to charge document preparation fees and, therefore, contrary state law purportedly prohibiting national banks from charging such fees as the unauthorized practice of law is preempted. Charter One Mortgage Corporation v. Kyle Condra, et al., No. 49A05-0501-CV-0030 (Indiana Court of Appeals).

- *Dodd–Frank Wall Street Reform and Consumer Protection Act of 2010.* The Dodd–Frank provisions addressing the federal preemption of state law: 1) preclude preemption of state law for national bank subsidiaries, agents, and affiliates; 2) change the "occupation of the field" preemption standard formerly applicable to federal savings associations to conform to the conflict preemption standard applicable to national banks; 3) affirm that the conflict preemption standard articulated in the Supreme Court's Barnett decision governs the preemption of state consumer financial laws; 4) set forth procedural and consultation requirements for certain preemption determinations going forward and clarify the criteria for judicial review of those determinations; and 5) address the authority of state attorneys general to enforce federal and state laws by codifying the Supreme Court's decision in the Cuomo case. OCC Interpretive Letter 1132 (May 12, 2011).

- *Exportation of Interest Rates by National Bank Operating Subsidiaries.* The OCC issued a letter confirming that a national bank operating subsidiary may export interest rates pursuant to 12 USC 85 under the same terms and conditions applicable to its parent national bank. Letter from Julie L. Williams to Costas Avrakatos, Esq., Kirkpatrick & Lockhart. OCC Interpretive Letter 954 (December 16, 2002).

- *Exportation of Rates.* National banks located in more than one state may export interest rates (including any fees in connection with credit extension or availability) from one state to customers in another state. This "most-favored-lender" status allows national bank to export these rates from its main office state to customers in any state with no restrictions, and from a branch office state if certain conditions are met. 12 USC 85; 12 CFR 7.4001; Smiley v. Citibank, 517 US 735 (1996); OCC Interpretive Letter No. 803, reprinted in [1997 Transfer Binder] Fed. Banking L. Rep. (CCH) ¶ 81,250 (October 7, 1997); OCC Interpretive Letter No. 782, reprinted in [1997 Transfer Binder] Fed. Banking L. Rep. (CCH) ¶ 81,209 (May 21, 1997).

- *Federal Branches: Illinois.* Illinois restrictions on the establishment of federal branches do not limit the authority of the Comptroller to license federal branches of foreign banks in Illinois. OCC Interpretive Letter No. 590, reprinted in [1992-1993 Transfer Binder] Fed. Banking L. Rep. (CCH) ¶ 83,415 (June 18, 1992).

- *Fee for Preparation of Bank Mortgage Documents.* A national bank does not engage in the unauthorized practice of law by charging a fee for preparing its own mortgage documents. The OCC filed an amicus brief supporting a national bank's argument that the National Bank Act and OCC regulations preempt Indiana law making it the unauthorized practice of law for lenders to charge document preparation fees in connection with their mortgage lending operations. Although the Indiana Court of Appeals rejected the bank's argument, the Indiana Supreme Court ultimately concluded that lenders could charge such fees without violating state law. Charter One Mortgage Corp. v. Condra, 865 N.E.2d 602 (Ind. 2007).

- *Fees and Charges.* National banks may establish noninterest charges and fees, including deposit account service charges and fees for other banking services, notwithstanding efforts by states or municipalities to restrict or limit national bank's fees and charges. 12 CFR 7.4002; Bank of America, N.A. v. San Francisco, No. C 99 4817 VRW (N.D. Ca.) (preliminary injunction granted November 15,1999).

- *Fiduciary Powers.* A national bank is authorized under federal law to be appointed, and accept any appointment, to act in a fiduciary capacity permitted to state fiduciaries in Missouri without obtaining any express qualification under Missouri law, including a reciprocity certificate. OCC Interpretive Letter No. 1080 (April 4, 2007).

- *Fiduciary Powers.* A national bank is authorized under federal law to be appointed, and accept any appointment, to act in a fiduciary capacity permitted to state fiduciaries in North Carolina without obtaining any express qualification or otherwise qualifying under North Carolina law. OCC Interpretive Letter No.1103 (September 18, 2008).

- *Fiduciary Powers.* A national bank is authorized under federal law to conduct fiduciary activities in the states of Georgia and South Carolina notwithstanding state laws that purport to limit the bank's ability to do so by requiring, among other things, that the bank be federally-insured and have a physical presence in the state. Letter also concludes that the bank may deposit the amount of securities required pursuant to federal law and the OCC's regulations rather than a conflicting amount required under Florida law. OCC Interpretive Letter No. 1106 (October 10, 2008).

- *Information-Sharing Among Affiliates.* The Ninth Circuit Court of Appeals held that the clause of the Fair Credit Reporting Act (FCRA) preempting state laws regulating the exchange of information among affiliates invalidates the requirements and prohibitions imposed by the California Financial Information Privacy Act (commonly known as SB1) with respect to affiliates sharing information bearing on a consumer's creditworthiness, credit standing, credit capacity, character, or other factor used to establish the consumer's eligibility for credit or insurance. American Bankers Ass'n

v. Gould, 412 F.3d 1081 (9th Cir. 2005). The Court remanded the case, however, to have the district court determine if any part of SB-1 survived preemption or could be severed. On remand, the district court concluded that FCRA preempts the affiliate-sharing provisions of SB-1, and that the Court lacked the power to modify the statute by severing the unconstitutional portions of those provisions. The Court, therefore, enjoined enforcement of those provisions of SB-1 that would require financial institutions to obtain permission from their customers before sharing certain customer information with their affiliates. American Bankers Ass'n v. Lockyer, WL 2452798 (E.D.Cal. Oct. 4, 2005).

- *Information Sharing With Affiliates.* The Fair Credit Reporting Act (FCRA) preempts state laws that impose restrictions on information- sharing with affiliates. The defendant municipalities withdrew their appeal to the Ninth Circuit of a U.S. District Court decision holding that provisions of the FCRA preempt ordinances that impose restrictions on the sharing of confidential consumer information between financial institutions and their affiliates. They repealed the ordinances that were the subject of the litigation and moved the court to dismiss the appeal as moot and to vacate the district court's order. The Ninth Circuit granted the motion, and the district court vacated its decision. Bank of America v. Daly City, Nos. C 02-4343 and C 02-4943 (N.D. Cal. 2003).

- *Insurance.* As a general rule, states may not prevent or restrict national banks or their affiliates from engaging in any activities authorized or permitted under GLBA. Specifically in the area of insurance sales, solicitations, or cross-marketing activities, any state laws outside 13 specific safe harbors may be struck down, if they are not consistent with the traditional preemption principles set forth by the U.S. Supreme Court in Barnett Bank of Marion County, N.A. v. Nelson 517 U.S. 25 (1996). 15 USC 6701 (as added by section 104 of the Gramm-Leach-Bliley Act); Valley National Bank v. Lavecchia, 59 F. Supp. 2d 432 (D. N.J. 1999); New York Bankers Association, Inc. v. Levin, 999 F. Supp. 716 (W.D. N.Y. 1998); Texas Bankers Association v. Bomer, 1997 U.S. Dist. LEXIS 13422 (W.D. Tex. August 7, 1997).

- *Insurance Law Under the Gramm-Leach-Bliley Act, Massachusetts.* The OCC published its opinion that certain provisions of the Massachusetts Consumer Protection Act Relative to the Sale of Insurance by Banks are preempted under insurance preemption standards established by section 104 of the Gramm-Leach-Bliley Act. Specifically, federal law preempts the provisions of Massachusetts law that purport to prohibit: 1) nonlicensed bank personnel from referring a prospective customer to a licensed insurance agent or broker except upon an inquiry initiated by the customer; 2) a bank from compensating an employee for such a referral; and 3) a bank from telling a loan applicant that insurance products are available through the bank until the application is approved and, in the case of a loan secured by a mortgage on real property, until after the customer has accepted the bank's written commitment to extend credit. Preemption Determination, *Federal Register*, 67 FR 13405 (March 22, 2002). The Massachusetts Insurance Commissioner filed a petition in the First Circuit seeking review of that OCC preemption letter. The court dismissed the petition, holding that the dispute between the OCC and the commissioner was insufficient to create a justiciable case or controversy and should be deemed to fall outside the scope of the statutory provisions for judicial review. Bowler v. Hawke, 320 F.3d 59 (1st Cir. 2003).

– *Insurance Law Under the Gramm-Leach-Bliley Act, West Virginia.* The state of West Virginia and the state insurance commissioner filed a petition with the U.S. Court of Appeals for the Fourth Circuit seeking a review of an OCC preemption determination opining that certain provisions of the West Virginia Insurance Sales Consumer Protection Act are preempted by the National Bank Act. In an unpublished opinion, a majority of the panel held that the petitioners had standing to bring the suit, that the OCC had implicit authority under the Gramm-Leach-Bliley Act to issue its preemption opinion, and that the statutes were preempted by the National Bank Act. One of the judges dissented on the ground that the petition presented no justiciable case or controversy. Petitioners filed a petition for rehearing, which the OCC was ordered to answer, and which was ultimately denied. Cline v. Hawke, 51 Fed. Appx. 392 (4th Cir. 2002).

– *Interest Rates and Fees.* Interest rates and fees constituting interest that may be imposed under 12 USC 85 by a national bank operating subsidiary permissibly may be based on the usury laws of the parent bank's home state under circumstances where parent bank may charge home state rates, even though the operating subsidiary has no offices in that home state. OCC Interpretive Letter No. 1100 (May 5, 2008).

– *Limits on Sales of Reclaimed Leased Vehicles.* Certain provisions of Ohio law that purport to limit the ability of national banks to engage in the business of leasing automobiles are preempted. As interpreted by the Ohio Bureau of Motor Vehicles, Ohio law prohibits the public sale of reclaimed leased vehicles. Direct sales to the public are permitted in the case of repossessed vehicles, but vehicles reclaimed from a lessor for non- payment are not considered "repossessed" under Ohio law. As a result, national banks would be required to sell reclaimed leased vehicles at wholesale to persons licensed as dealers under state law. These requirements frustrate the ability of national banks to operate efficiently and in a manner consistent with safe and sound banking practices, and therefore would be preempted. Preemption determination, *Federal Register*, 66 FR 23977 (May 10, 2001).

– *Loan Production Offices: Texas.* A Texas regulation requiring licensing of loan production offices as a condition for operation, and regulating the types of activities that can be conducted at such offices, is preempted. OCC Interpretive Letter (May 15, 1995).

– *Mandatory Disclosures to Credit Card Holders.* A U.S. District Court held that the National Bank Act preempts California laws requiring compliance with certain combinations of warnings to credit card holders regarding the possible consequences of paying only the minimum amount each month. OCC filed an amicus brief.

American Bankers Association v. Lockyer, 239 F. Supp.2d 1000, 2002 WL 31941511 (E.D. Cal. 2002).

– *Miller v. Bank of America.* The California Supreme Court upheld the lower appellate court decision reversing a trial court class-action judgment that granted monetary and injunctive relief to account-holders whose overdrafts and overdraft fees had been recouped by the bank from subsequently deposited public benefit payments (such as SSI benefits). The California Supreme Court held that this common account balancing practice did not violate California law. The U.S. Department of Justice, which represented the OCC, the U.S. Treasury, and the U.S. Social Security Administration, filed an amicus brief arguing that the state law was preempted by the National Bank Act and OCC regulations and would have adverse consequences for Treasury and Social Security programs. Miller v. Bank of America, 46 Cal.4th 630, 207 P.3d 531, 94 Cal.Rptr.3d 31 (Cal. 2009).

– *Mortgage Loan Restrictions: Pennsylvania.* Residential mortgage loan terms prescribed by the Pennsylvania Banking Code do not apply to national banks (applying former 12 CFR 34.2), and Pennsylvania state- chartered banks can choose to follow OCC regulations instead of state law (applying 12 USC 3803). OCC Interpretive Letter (September 30, 1992).

– *Mortgage Operating Subsidiaries.* United States courts of appeal for four circuits have upheld decisions by district courts in California, Connecticut, Maryland, and Michigan, that granted national banks declaratory and injunctive relief in suits challenging states' efforts to license and exercise visitorial powers over the operating subsidiaries of national banks. In each case, the United States courts of appeal affirmed district court decisions that the National Bank Act and OCC regulations preempt state licensing and enforcement authority over the real estate lending activities of national bank operating subsidiaries. Wachovia Bank, N.A. v. Burke, 414 F.3d 305 (2nd Cir.) petition for cert. filed; 74 U.S.L.W. 3223 (U.S. September 30, 2005) (No. 05-431); Wells Fargo Bank, N.A. v. Boutris, 419 F.3d 949 (9th Cir. 2005); Wachovia Bank, N.A. v. Watters, 431 F.3d 556 (6th Cir. 2005), cert. granted 75 U.S.L.W. 3019 (U.S. June 19, 2006) (No. 05-1342); and Nat'l City Bank of Ind. v. Turnbaugh, 463 F.3d 325 (4th Cir. 2006), petition for cert. filed, 75 U.S.L.W. 3267 (U.S. November 7, 2006). Oral argument was held in Watters v. Wachovia, No. 05-1342, on November 29, 2006.

– *Motor Vehicle Sales Finance Laws.* Federal law preempts a Michigan statute, as interpreted by the Michigan Financial Institutions Bureau, that would limit the ability of national banks to use agents to make loans to finance motor vehicle sales. The state law would have had the effect of prohibiting national banks from charging interest at a rate permitted by their home state as authorized by 12 USC 85, and would have imposed a licensing requirement on national banks as a precondition to exercising permissible federal powers. Preemption determination, *Federal Register*, 66 FR 28593 (May 23, 2001).

- *Multistate Fiduciary Operations.* The OCC issued a letter to a national bank that concluded that (i) a national bank's trust powers are governed by federal law and derive from 12 USC 92a and Part 9 of the OCC's regulations; (ii) a national bank looks to the law of the state in which it acts in a fiduciary capacity in order to determine which capacities are permissible for the bank to act in for customers in that state as well as other states; and (iii) a state's authority to regulate instrumentalities of its own government (for example, by enacting state laws restricting the types of trustees, or other fiduciaries, those state government instrumentalities may appoint) does not affect the fiduciary authorities granted to national banks as a matter of federal law. OCC Interpretive Letter No. 973 (August 12, 2003).

- *Multistate Fiduciary Operations.* A national bank has the authority to implement a national fiduciary program. Pursuant to the OCC's regulations at 12 CFR 9.7(e)(2), any state law, other than a law made applicable by 12 USC 92a, that limits or establishes preconditions on the exercise of the fiduciary powers that are to be exercised as part of the bank's program are not applicable to the bank. Finally, while a national bank may have the federal authority to act in various fiduciary capacities in a given state, that authority does not determine whether a state instrumentality has authority under its governing state statutes to contract with the national bank for fiduciary services. OCC Interpretive Letter No. 995 (June 22, 2004).

- *Naming and Advertising of Branch Facilities: Texas.* A Texas regulation concerning the "naming and advertising of branch facilities" is not preempted for national banks. OCC Interpretive Letter No. 674, reprinted in [1994-1995 Transfer Binder] Fed. Banking L. Rep. (CCH) 83,622 (June 9, 1995).

- *National, Nonnational Branch Operations.* National banks may establish nationwide loan production offices (LPO), deposit production offices (DPO), ATMs, remote service units (RSU), and other nonbranch facilities, notwithstanding any state laws that attempt to regulate the location or operation of, or to impose licensing requirements on, those facilities. ATMs are excluded from the definition of a branch by statute. 12 USC 36(j), 1813(o). LPOs, DPOs, RSUs, and other nonbranch offices do not constitute branches under OCC interpretations and/or court decisions. Bank One, Utah v. Guttau, 190 F.3d 844 (8th Cir. 1999); 12 CFR 7.4003-4005.

- *New York State Attorney General Barred From Enforcing Subpoenas for Mortgage Loan Records of National Banks.* The Second Circuit Court of Appeals upheld federal district court decisions barring the New York State Attorney General from enforcing subpoenas for mortgage loan records of national banks to investigate compliance with state fair lending statutes. The New York Attorney General had appealed two related federal district court decisions in suits brought by the OCC and the New York Clearing House Association in which the court enjoined the attorney general from:

  1) issuing subpoenas or demanding inspection of the books and records of any national banks for his investigation into residential lending practices,

2) instituting any enforcement actions to compel compliance with existing information demands, 3) instituting actions in court to enforce state fair lending laws; and 4) instituting a parens patriae action to enforce the federal Fair Housing Act. The Second Circuit upheld in its entirety the district court decision in the suit brought by the OCC, but vacated the decision in the Clearing House case regarding the Fair Housing Act upon concluding that the district court lacked jurisdiction because the issue was not yet ripe for review. The New York Attorney General has petitioned the Second Circuit to grant en banc review of the panel's decision. Clearing House Association, LLC, Office of the Comptroller of the Currency v. Cuomo, 510 F.3d 105 (2d Cir. 2007).

– *Non-Accountholder Fee to Cash an Official Check.* A national bank is authorized pursuant to 12 USC 24(Seventh) and 12 CFR 7.4002 to establish and charge a fee to a non-accountholder customer for the service of cashing an official check. OCC Interpretive Letter No. 1094 (February 27, 2008).

– *Not Sufficient Funds (NSF) Fees.* A national bank has authority, pursuant to 12 USC 24(Seventh) and 12 CFR 7.4002, to charge NSF fees when the fee resulted, in part, from the bank's policy of posting checks in order from the highest to the lowest amount. Letter from Julie L. Williams to John D. Wright, Vice President and Assistant General Counsel, Wells Fargo Bank (April 15, 2002).

– *Ohio Insurance Law.* A unanimous panel of the U.S. Court of Appeals for the Sixth Circuit, affirming the court below, held that 12 USC 92 preempts provisions of Ohio law that interfered with a national bank's power to sell insurance as agent in Ohio. The specific Ohio law provisions at issue were the Ohio "principal purpose test" and corporate organizational requirements that have the effect of significantly hindering a national bank's sale of insurance in Ohio. The case was remanded to the district court to address the issue of what effect, if any, the preemption provisions in the Gramm-Leach-Bliley Act have on the preemption analysis. The OCC filed amicus briefs with both the district and appellate courts. Association of Banks in Insurance v. Duryee, No. 99-3917 (6th Cir.) (November 1, 2001).

– *"On Us" Check Cashing Fees.* National banks may charge a nonaccountholder a convenience fee for using a bank teller to cash an "on us" check. An "on us" check is a check drawn on the bank by one of the bank's customers. The fee is essentially compensating the bank for making cash immediately available to the payee; otherwise the payee would have to wait for the check to clear through the payment system. The U.S. Court of Appeals for the Fifth Circuit, affirming a decision below, held that the National Bank Act, specifically, 12 USC 24(Seventh), preempts state law prohibiting the charging of fees for cashing on-us checks. Wells Fargo v. James, 321 F.3d 488 (5th Cir. 2003). The OCC participated as amicus in the litigation.

– *"On Us" Check Cashing Fees.* A national bank has authority, pursuant to 12 USC 24(Seventh) and 12 CFR 7.4002, to charge fees for the service of cashing checks drawn the bank and payable to non-accountholders of the bank. Letter from Julie L.

Williams to John H. Huffstutler, Esq., Associate General Counsel, Bank of America Legal Department (October 8, 2002); and Letter from Julie L. Williams to J. Thomas Cardwell, Esquire, Akerman, Senterfitt & Eidson, P.A. (April 4, 2002).

– *"On Us" Check Cashing Fees*. National banks may charge a nonaccountholder a convenience fee for using a bank teller to cash an "on us" check. An "on us" check is a check drawn on the bank by one of the bank's customers. The fee is essentially compensating the bank for making cash immediately available to the payee; otherwise the payee would have to wait for the check to clear through the payment system. A U.S. District Court, with which the OCC filed an amicus brief, held that the National Bank Act, specifically, 12 USC 24(Seventh), preempts state law prohibiting the charging of fees for cashing on-us checks. Bank of America v. Sorrell, Case No. 1:02 CV 1518 (GET)(N.D. Ga.). Earlier, another U.S. District Court issued a similar ruling as to a Texas state law prohibition on these fees. Wells Fargo v. James, Case No. 01-CA-538- JRN (W.D. Tex.), aff'd 321 F.3d 488, 5th Cir. No. 01-51298 (2003). The OCC participated as amicus in that litigation as well.

– *"On Us" Check Cashing Fees*. The federal district court for the western district of Texas granted a permanent injunction restraining the effectiveness of a new Texas statute purporting to prohibit banks from charging a teller's fee for cashing a check drawn on an account with that bank (i.e., an "on us" check cashing fee). The case was brought by several banks against the Texas banking commissioner. The OCC filed a brief amicus curie in favor of the plaintiff's position. Wells Fargo Bank Texas v. Randall James, No. 01-CA-538-JRN (U.S.D.C., W.D. Tex.) (December 3, 2001).

– *Out-of-State Banks (Restrictions on Branching): Idaho*. An Idaho statute prohibiting out-of-state national banks from branching in Idaho, as permitted by federal law, is preempted. Corporate Decision 95-59 (November 20, 1995).

– *Out-of-State Banks (Restrictions on Branching): Kansas*. A Kansas statute prohibiting out-of-state national banks from branching in Kansas, as permitted by federal law, is preempted. Corporate Decision 95-05, reprinted in [1994-1995 Transfer Binder] Fed. Banking L. Rep. (CCH) 90,474 (February 16, 1995).

– *Out-of-State Banks (Restrictions on Branching): Maryland*. A Maryland statute prohibiting out-of-state national banks from branching in Maryland, as permitted by federal law, is preempted. Corporate Decision 95-10 (March 8, 1995).

– *Out-of-State Banks (Restrictions on Branching): Texas*. Texas statutes that purport to prohibit an out-of-state national bank from having branches in Texas acquired pursuant to federal law are preempted. Corporate Decision 98-07, 99 OCC QJ LEXIS 22 (January 15, 1998).

– *Out-of-State Banks (Restrictions on Fiduciary Activities): Missouri*. Missouri statutes that prohibit an out-of-state national bank from exercising fiduciary powers in

Missouri are preempted. Corporate Decision 98-16, 99 OCC QJ LEXIS 22 (March 4, 1998).

– *Out-of-State Banks (Restrictions on Fiduciary Activity): Wisconsin.* A Wisconsin statute that prohibits an out-of-state national bank from acting as fiduciary is preempted. Corporate Decision 97-33, 98 OCC QJ LEXIS 6 (June 1, 1997).

– *Out-of-State Banks (Restrictions on Interstate Mergers, Transacting Business): Texas.* A Texas statute that purports to prohibit interstate mergers under the Riegle-Neal Act is preempted as to a merger authorized under other federal law (e.g., merger of an out-of-state national bank with branches in Texas and an in-state national bank pursuant to 12 USC 215(a). In addition, a Texas constitutional provision that appears to prohibit out-of-state national banks from conducting business in Texas and a statute that prohibits out-of-state national banks from conducting fiduciary activities in Texas are preempted. Corporate Decision 98-19 (April 2, 1998).

– *Out-of-State Banks (Restrictions on Relocation): Kansas.* A Kansas statute prohibiting out-of-state national banks owned by bank holding companies from relocating into Kansas, as permitted by federal law, is preempted. Corporate Decision 95-28 (April 4, 1995).

– *Out-of-State Banks (Restrictions on Transacting Business): Kentucky.* A Kentucky statute prohibiting out-of-state national banks from transacting business in Kentucky is preempted. Corporate Decision 95-13 (March 14, 1995).

– *Out-of-State Banks (Restrictions on Transacting Business): West Virginia.* A West Virginia statute prohibiting out-of-state national banks from transacting business in West Virginia is preempted. Corporate Decision 95-24 (June 9, 1995).

– *Out-of-State Banks (Restrictions on Transacting Business): West Virginia.* A West Virginia statute prohibiting out-of-state national banks from transacting business in West Virginia is preempted. Corporate Decision 95-46 (September 11, 1995).

– *Out-of-State Banks (Restrictions on Transacting Business): West Virginia.* A West Virginia statute prohibiting out-of-state national banks from transacting business in West Virginia is preempted. Corporate Decision 96-06 (January 29, 1996).

– *Out-of-State Banks (Restrictions on Transacting Business, Branching): Connecticut.* Connecticut statutes prohibiting out-of-state national banks from transacting business in Connecticut, unless permitted under state law, requiring state approval for the merger of an out-of-state national bank with a Connecticut bank, and requiring state approval for branching in Connecticut by an out-of-state national bank, as permitted by federal law, are preempted. Corporate Decision 96-17 (March 27, 1996).

– *Out-of-State Banks (Restrictions on Transacting Business, Branching): West Virginia, Ohio).* A West Virginia statute prohibiting out-of-state national banks from transacting business in West Virginia is preempted and an Ohio law prohibiting out-of-state national banks from branching in Ohio, as permitted by federal law, is preempted. Corporate Decision 95-50 (October 5, 1995).

– *Out-of-State Banks (Restrictions on Transacting Business, Mergers, and Branching): Connecticut.* Connecticut statutes prohibiting out-of-state national banks from transacting business in Connecticut, unless permitted under state law, requiring state approval for the merger of an out-of-state national bank with a Connecticut bank, and requiring state approval for branching in Connecticut by an out-of-state national bank, as permitted by federal law, are preempted. Corporate Decision 95-34 (July 26, 1995).

– *Overdraft Practices.* A national bank is federally authorized to honor overdrafts and charge fees for doing so. These practices do not implicate the OCC's rules concerning state laws pertaining to the "right to collect debts." OCC Interpretive Letter No. 1082 (May 17, 2007).

– *Prepayment Fees.* National banks can charge prepayment fees to the same extent as federal savings associations under 12 USC 85 and the Michigan parity statute that allows state banks to charge prepayment fees to the same extent as federal savings associations. OCC Interpretive Letter No. 1004 (August 4, 2004).

– *Real Estate Loans; ARMs.* National banks may make real estate loans under 12 USC 371 and 12 CFR 34.3 without regard to state law limitations concerning: (a) the amount of a loan in relation to the appraised value of the real estate, (b) the loan repayment schedule, (c) the term to maturity of the loan, (d) the amount of funds that may be loaned upon the security of the real estate, and (e) the covenants and restrictions that are required to qualify the leasehold as acceptable security for a real estate loan (12 CFR 34.4). In addition, national banks and their subsidiaries may make, sell, purchase, participate in, or otherwise deal in ARM loans and interests therein without regard to any state law limitations on those activities. 12 CFR 34.21.

– *Registrations, Fee Requirements, Mortgage Broker or Lender: Georgia.* Provisions of the Georgia Residential Mortgage Act that impose registration and fee requirements as a condition to transacting business directly or indirectly as mortgage brokers or mortgage lenders are preempted. OCC Interpretive Letter No. 644, reprinted in [1994 Transfer Binder] Fed. Banking L. Rep. (CCH) ¶ 83,593 (March 24, 1994).

– *Registrations, Investment Advisor: Texas.* A Texas statute that requires a national bank to register with the state as an investment adviser before providing investment advisory services to its trust customers is preempted. OCC Interpretive Letter No. 628, reprinted in [1993-1994 Transfer Binder] Fed. Banking L. Rep. (CCH) ¶ 83,511 (July 19, 1993).

– *Sale of Authorized Stored Value Cards.* States may not interfere with a national bank's sale of authorized stored value cards with particular features by prohibiting third-party agents from performing services for the bank. The First Circuit Court of Appeals upheld a district court decision that the National Bank Act preempts a state law that purports to prohibit a national bank from using a shopping mall operator to market and deliver to retail customers the national bank's gift cards that carry an expiration date and dormancy fee. The district court and court of appeals rejected the state's argument that, because the bank was free to sell its gift cards to customers through other means, the state statute regulated only the conduct of the mall operator, not the bank. The Supreme Court denied the New Hampshire Attorney Generals petition for certiorari on the Supreme Court. SPGGC LLC v. Ayotte, 488 F.3d 525 (1st Cir. 2007).

- *Sale of Insurance*. A U.S. District Court granted summary judgment to plaintiffs who challenged as preempted state statutory provisions that restrict national bank insurance sales, solicitation, and cross marketing. The court held that section 104 of the Gramm-Leach-Bliley Act, 15 USC 6701, preempts state laws that restrict the insurance sales activities of national banks. Massachusetts Banking Ass'n v. Bowler, 392 F.Supp.2d 24 (D.Mass. 2005).

- *State Anti-Discrimination Laws*. State anti-discrimination laws are generally not preempted by the OCC's new preemption rule. OCC Interpretive Letter No. 998 (March 9, 2004).

- *State Insurance Sales Law Under the Gramm-Leach-Bliley Act*. The Commonwealth of Massachusetts and its Commissioners of Insurance and Banks filed a petition with the U.S. Court of Appeals for the First Circuit seeking review of an OCC preemption determination opining that provisions of a state consumer protection statute regulating insurance sales, solicitations, and cross-marketing activities of banks in Massachusetts were preempted by the Gramm-Leach-Bliley Act. The panel held that the OCC's opinion letter did not give rise to a regulatory conflict between state and federal regulators meeting the "case and controversy" requirement for judicial review. Bowler v. Hawke, 320 F. 3d 59 (1st Cir. 2003). In an earlier opinion, the majority of a Fourth Circuit panel, facing essentially the same scenario, held that the state of West Virginia and the state insurance commissioner had standing to bring the suit, that the OCC had implicit authority under the GLBA to preempt state statutes, and that the statutes were preempted. One of the judges dissented and found lack of standing. Cline v. Hawke, 51 Fed. Appx. 392 (4th Cir. 2002), cert. denied, Independent Ins. Agents and Brokers of America v. Hawke, 124 S.Ct. 63 (2003).

- *State Insurance Sales Law Under the Gramm-Leach-Bliley Act*. Certain provisions of West Virginia's Insurance Sales Consumer Protection Act are preempted under insurance preemption standards established by section 104 of the Gramm-Leach-Bliley Act. Federal law preempts some, but not all, of the provisions of the West Virginia Act. In particular, federal law does not preempt the following provisions of the West Virginia Act with respect to national banks:

- The prohibition against requiring or implying that the purchase of an insurance product from a bank is required as a condition of a loan;

- The prohibition against a bank offering an insurance product in combination with other products unless all of the products are available separately; and
- The requirement that, when insurance is required as a condition of obtaining a loan, the insurance and credit transactions be completed independently and through separate documents.

The following provisions of the act are preempted only in part:

- The provisions prescribing the content of the disclosures that a bank is required to make in connection with the solicitation of an insurance product and the requirement that a bank that sells insurance obtain a written acknowledgment, in a separate document, from its insurance customer that certain disclosures were provided are not preempted.

- However, the provisions regarding the manner and timing of certain required disclosures are preempted.

And the following provisions are preempted:

- The requirement that banks use separate employees for insurance solicitations;

- The restrictions on the timing of bank employees' referral or solicitation of insurance business from customers who have loan applications pending with the bank;

- The restrictions on sharing with bank affiliates information acquired by a financial institution in the course of a loan transaction to solicit or offer insurance; and

- The requirement that banks segregate the place of solicitation or sale of insurance so that it is readily distinguishable as separate and distinct from the deposit taking and lending areas. Preemption determination, *Federal Register*, 66 FR 51502 (October 9, 2001).

- *State Law Regulation of Mortgage Operating Subsidiary.* The U.S. District Court for Connecticut, in granting the bank's motion for summary judgment, held that 12 CFR 7.4006 preempts state laws that purport to impose on national bank operating subsidiaries a state regulatory regime requiring businesses engaged in the making of first and second mortgages to obtain a state license and subjecting them to enforcement proceedings by the Connecticut Banking Commissioner. Wachovia Bank, N.A. v. Burke, 319 F.Supp.2d 275 (D. Conn., May 25, 2004). In a separate case, the U.S. District Court for the Western District of Michigan, in granting the bank's motion for summary judgment, held that 12 CFR 7.4006 preempts state law that purports to authorize the Michigan banking commissioner to require national bank operating subsidiaries to obtain a state license in order to engage in the business of making of first and second mortgages on behalf of its parent bank. Wachovia Bank, N.A. v. Watters, 334 F.Supp.2d 957 (W.D. Mich., August 30, 2004).

- *State Law Restricting Balloon Payment Loans.* A state law that places restrictions on the terms of loans with balloon payment features is preempted with respect to a national bank and its operating subsidiaries. OCC Interpretive Letter No. 1015 (September 20, 2004).

- *State Unclaimed Property and Escheat Laws.* An OCC letter to the National Association of State Treasurers (NAST) and the National Association of Unclaimed Property Administrators (NAUPA) clarifies that the OCC's preemption and visitorial powers regulations do not change existing standards, established by U.S. Supreme Court precedent and federal statute, that govern the applicability and enforcement of state unclaimed property and escheat laws. OCC Interpretive Letter No. 1006 (August 19, 2004).

- *Subordinate Lien Mortgage Origination.* Part 34 and the OCC's past preemption opinions preempt section 24-4.5-3-402 of the Indiana Code when originating subordinate lien mortgages. OCC Interpretive Letter No. 1015 (September 20, 2004).

- *Sunday Operation: Alabama.* Alabama law prohibiting Sunday operations is preempted. OCC Interpretive Letter No. 706, reprinted in [1995-1996 Transfer Binder] Fed. Banking L. Rep. (CCH) ¶ 81,021 (January 18, 1996).

- *Supreme Court Affirmation of Ruling That Federal Law Preempts Michigan's Restrictions on the Activities of National Bank Mortgage Operating Subsidiaries.* The Court affirmed that the National Bank Act preempts state laws that would require national bank operating subsidiaries to obtain state licenses to engage in banking activities authorized for their parent national banks and that the National Bank Act prohibits states from exercising any "visitorial" powers over operating subsidiaries of national banks. The case heard by the Supreme Court was one of four cases in which U.S. courts of appeal upheld decisions by district courts in California, Connecticut, Maryland, and Michigan that granted national banks declaratory and injunctive relief in suits challenging states' efforts to license and exercise enforcement authority over national bank mortgage subsidiaries. After issuing its ruling in the Michigan case, the Supreme Court denied petitions for Supreme Court review filed by Connecticut and Maryland. Watters v. Wachovia Bank, N.A., U.S., 127 S.Ct. 1559 (2007).

- *Trust Operations.* State laws that prohibit or restrict national banks from soliciting, conducting, or operating a trust business through nonbranch trust offices are preempted. This enables national banks to conduct a nationwide trust business notwithstanding branching requirements or state law prohibitions, restrictions, or licensing requirements in states in which the activities are being conducted through nonbranch offices. 12 USC 92a; OCC Interpretive Letters Nos. 872, reprinted in

[Current Transfer Binder] Fed. Banking L. Rep. (CCH) ¶ 81,366 (October 28, 1999); and 866, reprinted in [Current Transfer Binder] Fed. Banking L. Rep. (CCH) 81,360 (October 8, 1999).

- *Uniform Commercial Code.* An OCC letter to the National Conference of Commissioners on Uniform State Laws (NCCUSL) and the American Law Institute (ALI) clarifies the scope of the final preemption rule. It confirms the conclusions of NCCUSL and ALI that the Uniform Commercial Code (UCC) does not "obstruct, impair, or condition" the ability of national banks to exercise fully the powers granted by federal law; and those powers are implemented and supported by the UCC, which provides a uniform law of general applicability on which parties rely in their daily commercial transactions. OCC Interpretive Letter No. 1005 (June 10, 2004).

- *Use of Third Party to Market National Bank Stored Value Cards.* The United States District Court for New Hampshire ruled on August 1, 2006, that the National Bank Act preempts state restrictions on fees and expiration dates on gift cards sold by a national bank and permits a national bank to use a third party that owns and operates shopping malls to market and deliver the bank's gift cards to customers. SPGGC, LLC; MetaBank; and U.S. Bank, N.A. v. Ayotte, 443 F.Supp.2d 197 (D. N.H. 2006), appeal docketed No. 06-2326 (1st Cir. September 21, 2006).

- *Usury: Arkansas.* A usury provision in the Arkansas constitution applies to national banks in the same manner as it applies to state banks, and therefore is not preempted. Letter from Peter Liebesman, Assistant Director, Legal Advisory Services Division (June 10, 1992).

- *Visitation, in General.* In general, only the OCC may exercise visitorial powers with respect to a national bank, such as conducting examinations, inspecting or requiring the production of books or records, or prosecuting enforcement actions. For that reason, except in the limited circumstances in which federal law grants express special authority to a state or other federal official, national banks have only one regulator, the OCC. 12 CFR 7.4000; National State Bank, Elizabeth, New Jersey v. Long, 630 F.2d 981 (3d Cir. 1980); First Union National Bank v. Burke, 48 F. Supp. 2d 132 (D. Conn. 1999). The following are examples of preemption in connection with visitation:

  o *Visitation, Insurance Agency: New York.* New York law permitting state inspection of books and records of a national bank's insurance agency to determine compliance with applicable state law is not preempted. Letter (July 7, 1997).

  o *Visitation, Licensing, Brokerage: Iowa.* Provisions of the Iowa Uniform Securities Act requiring national banks performing discount brokerage activities to register with the state, and providing for state examination, are preempted. Letter (December 7, 1992).

o *Visitation, Licensing, Credit Card Operations: Idaho, Wisconsin, and Wyoming.* Portions of the Idaho Credit Code (requiring credit card issuers, including national banks, to obtain licenses to issue credit cards to Idaho residents, and to be subject to visitation or enforcement by state officials), the Wisconsin Consumer Act (requiring national banks making certain consumer credit transactions to comply with notification requirements and to submit to visitation and enforcement by state officials), and the Wyoming Uniform Consumer Credit Code (containing similar visitation and enforcement provisions) are preempted. OCC Interpretive Letter No. 614 (January 15, 1993).

o *Visitation, Registration, Securities Brokerage: Nebraska.* Portions of the Nebraska Securities Act requiring national banks performing securities brokerage activities to register, and providing for state examination, are preempted. OCC Interpretive Letter (February 1, 1993).

o *Visitation, Subpoena: Texas.* A subpoena issued by the Texas House of Representatives seeking national bank books and records represents an attempted exercise of visitorial powers by state authorities and is therefore preempted. OCC Interpretive Letter (June 3, 1993).

– *Visitorial Powers, New York Attorney General.* OCC filed suit against the State of New York Attorney General (NYAG) in District Court seeking injunctive relief to prevent the NYAG from interfering with the OCC's exclusive visitorial authority over the banking activities of national banks and their operating subsidiaries. On the same day, the New York Clearing House filed a similar suit for injunctive relief against the New York Attorney General. On October 12, 2005, the Court issued an opinion and order granting the OCC the requested injunctive relief. The Court found that Attorney General Eliot Spitzer's assertion of authority to investigate the real estate lending practices of national banks and their operating subsidiaries and to enforce their compliance with state law conflicts with 12 USC 484, as implemented by 12 CFR 7.4000, and therefore, is preempted by federal law. In the related case by the Clearing House, the Court granted plaintiff the same injunctive relief granted to the OCC and further relief prohibiting the Attorney General from bringing an action under the Fair Housing Act in the state's parens patriae capacity to enforce the FHA's fair lending provisions against the Clearing House's national bank members or their operating subsidiaries. On November 4, 2005, Eliot Spitzer filed appeals in both actions. The Office of the Comptroller of the Currency v. Spitzer, 396 F.Supp.2d 383 (S.D.N.Y 2005) and The Clearing House Association L.L.C. v. Spitzer, 394 F.Supp. 2d 620 (S.D.N.Y 2005), appeals docketed Nos. 05-6001 (2d Cir. November 8, 2005) and 05-5996 (2d Cir. November 7, 2005).

– *Visitorial Powers Over Mortgage Operating Subsidiaries.* Three U.S. courts of appeals and the U.S. district court for Maryland ruled that states are not permitted to require licenses from or exercise visitorial powers over the operating subsidiaries of national banks. In each case, the courts held that the National Bank Act and OCC regulations preempt state licensing and enforcement authority over the real estate lending activities of national bank operating subsidiaries. The Second, Sixth, and Ninth Circuits affirmed district court decisions handed down in 2004. Wachovia Bank, N.A. v. Burke, 414 F.3d 305 (2d Cir. 2005; Wachovia Bank, N.A. v. Watters, 431 F.3d 556 (6th Cir. 2005); and Wells Fargo v. Boutris, 419 F.3d 949 (9th Cir. 2005). The decision of U.S. district court in National City Bank of Indiana v. Turnbaugh, 367 F. Supp. 2d 805 (D. Md. 2005), is pending appeal in the Fourth Circuit. National City Bank of Indiana v. Turnbaugh, No. 05-1647 (4th Cir. appeal docketed June 13, 2005).

– *Visitorial Powers Over National Bank Operating Subsidiaries.* An interpretive letter explains OCC supervision of operating subsidiaries of national bank and the applicability of state law to operating subsidiaries. OCC Interpretive Letter No. 971 (January 16, 2003). In two separate decisions, a U.S. District Court held that only the OCC may exercise visitorial authority over the operating subsidiary of a national bank, and that the Depository Institutions Deregulatory and Monetary Control Act (DIDMCA) preempts state law that prohibits a home mortgage lender from receiving interest for more than one day prior to the date that the mortgage is recorded. Wells Fargo, N.A. v. Boutris, 252 F.Supp.2d 1065 (E.D. Cal. 2003); National City Bank of Indiana v. Boutris, 2003 WL 21536818 (E.D. Cal. July 2, 2003).

– *Visitorial Powers; State Licensing.* An operating subsidiary of a national bank is not required to be licensed under California law in order to engage in mortgage lending in the state. OCC Interpretive Letter No. 957 (January 27, 2003).